HIS LIVING WORD

He Speaks:
Wisdom—Comfort—Correction

Spoken to and
Recorded by
WILLIAM G. MASON

Compiled and Edited
By
Freda A. Coyner

Illustrated by
BARBARA BOSWORTH
www.heirlooms-gallery.com

BOOK 2 IN: HIS LIVING WORD SERIES

KWAY PUBLICATIONS ™

Copyright© 2011 by William Mason

HIS LIVING WORD

FROM "HIS LIVING WORD" SERIES

By William G. Mason

Printed in the United States of America

ISBN 978-1-4507-6913-6

Unless otherwise indicated, Bible quotations are taken from the New International Version.

Kway Publications **TM**

"There is always a Godly lesson in everything that happens to us. Learn from it, then pass the lesson on to others that cross your path!"

William G. Mass

iii

ACKNOWLEDGEMENT

Words go begging when it comes to the long tedious hours spent by my good friend and Christian sister, Freda Coyner, my Editor, who exhibited *stick-to-it* determination in bringing Book 2 to print-ready status for publishing in the "His Living Word Series."

In this labor of love she has spent long hours on all the details inherent in editing in order to assemble this 2nd book in the series of the Lord's messages spoken to my inner man (spirit), readying these materials for publication and distribution so that the public may read and enjoy our Lord's messages to a broken and dying world.

William G. Mason

WILLIAM MASON-- a bit of history.

I was born during the "Great depression" years to a Hebrew family. I never learned the language, but my parents observed the holidays as they came along.

I always had an appetite for learning new things, and also a built in creative mind; I was always in the top third of my class, which put me with the group who were preparing for a higher education.

I went to Case School of Applied Sciences. When World War II broke out, I applied for flight school and passed all the tests required by The United States Navy. By the time I finished flight training the war was almost ended; and after a freak aircraft accident in Norman, Oklahoma, I was discharged.

I came home, finished school, and was trained to be an Electro/Mechanical Research and Development Engineer after which I worked for Rockedyne in California designing circuit boards that went into Army and Navy ships and aircraft.

I met the love of my life at a dance hall in California and we were subsequently married March 31, 1951.

I traveled extensively during those years, calling on foreign clients for Rockedyne, straightening out technical problems for our company.

On one occasion, my company sent me to Japan: I was not a happy camper as I didn't, and still don't, like to travel alone that length of time. My chief engineer said, "Take your wife with you."

So off we went for three weeks. While in the air I said to Jean, "I think the Lord is saying something to me"—Jean said, "What is He saying?" I said, "I have a pen but nothing to write on!"

She leaned forward to the back pocket of the seat in front of her and said, "Here's a barf bag."

I only wrote three sentences; that is all I could hear at that time. I still have a yellowed envelope that was written in 1979. Since then the Lord has "impregnated" me with the title of His messages and given me the scripture that goes along with the body of the work.

That started over 30 years ago and I am still writing down his messages.

My Editor, Freda Coyner, and I, spent countless hours bringing the first book to fruition. It was published by Xulon Press in May of 2010 and is available at Amazon.com and Barnes & Nobles book stores. The title of Book 1 is <u>His Word From Above</u>. Its format is a 365-day devotional book. This is Book 2 in the series and I am working on Book 3.

My beloved wife of 57 years passed away from ovarian cancer May 15, 2008, after the Lord and I kept her alive for 12 years; and she is now exploring all of the Lord's universe along with family and friends that have gone on before her!

William G. Mason   8-29-10

INTRODUCTION

MY GREATEST GIFT

The greatest gift God the Father and my wife (home in glory May 15, 2008) gave me was *the will to serve mankind by the books He has privileged me to write*---to be a living witness of His love and compassion for me-- my family and friends.

That is the legacy I hope to pass on to my children and all my grandchildren and great grandchild Charley.

The Lord has gifted me beyond measure with family and friends. I really am not alone, for---protected by my personal angel gifted to me by His divine grace---I have experienced His love and closeness every waking hour throughout the day. For this I praise Him!

Suffering in and for the name of Jesus, strongly grows one up in *believing* faith and trust in the Father as He transforms those who go through their personal time of suffering for Jesus into seasoned soldiers in the King of King's army, walking into any battle for the souls of Man and winning them over to Christ for their salvation and eternal life in Him.

We walk into the battle with the *sword of the Spirit,* which is the Word of God; but--we don't fight, for the battle is not ours—it is His!

William G. Mason

Christ Our Comfort

IN LOVING MEMORY OF JEAN MASON

A few of her sayings

"Lord, let me view the world and people through Your eyes."

The silence of God; at times
" I can trust His heart when I can't trace His hands."

"Grace gives us the opportunity to repent—not a license to Sin."

"He, Jesus, looked beyond my faults, and tended to my needs."

"We know ourselves by our intentions, but others know us by our actions; good or bad."

"Knowledge of the scriptures does not save one; obedience to the call of Christ does."

"We only learn to love by reaching out to others in need of love."

ABBA FATHER

Abba is the most family-oriented term in the Old Testament. God was sometimes seen as Father of the nation Israel, but it was Christ's revelation that all believers are individually children of God by redemption. In lesser sense, all people are children of God by *creation*, but in the sense of the model prayer, the "Our Father," only believers can claim that revealed relationship.

Abba, Father occurs three times in the New Testament, the Aramaic term being used with a translation. *Abba* is the *most intimate term* for Father, the first word a child would learn for "Daddy." This word indicates how close the Father wants His children to feel toward Him!

Abba is used once in the Gospels and twice by Paul.

Mark 14:36. In the Garden of Gethsemane, His "soul...deeply grieved to the point of death." Jesus prayed, "Abba! Father! All things are possible for you; remove this cup from Me; yet not what I *Will*, but what you *Will*." At this crisis in His ministry, facing betrayal by Judas and shameful death on the cross, the Lord reverted to the tender word He had first used at Mary and Joseph's knees: *Abba*.

Romans 8:14-16. In one of the most beloved chapters in the Bible, Paul relates a word He no doubt learned at His own Jewish mother's knee to the believer's acceptance as a mature son by *adoption, as well as a child by new* birth. These blessings come through the third person of the Trinity:

"For all who are being led by the Spirit of God, these are sons of God; for you have not received a spirit of slavery leading to fear again, but you have received a spirit of adoption as sons by which we *cry out, "Abba! Father!"* "The Spirit Himself bears witness with our spirit that we are children of God."

Galatians 4:6. Paul's other use is similar, only here son-ship is contrasted with slavery. We are not merely slaves of God, although we should serve on *that level* of *submission*; we are sons and daughters. As God's sons and daughters we can boldly say, "Abba! Father!"

PART ONE

A CALL TO MISSIONS

Mt. 10: 5-42
These twelve Jesus sent out . . "And if anyone
gives a cup of cold water to one of these little ones
because he is my disciple, I tell you the truth, he
will certainly not lose his reward."

Behold the city---look over its girth. Like crowded animals
they dwell. Midst the sheep and the lambs dwell wolves of
ill repute. Knaves, thieves---bottled magic gone sour.
Arise to the occasion. Your mission call awakens. My
Spirit within you comes forth to do battle with the enemy.
You have heard, "Many are called but few are chosen."
[Mt.22:16] You---you, My child, are not only called but
chosen to bear witness of My Glory wherever I send you;
for I know in My heart of hearts that you set no defense
against My Spirit.
I know that you have sacrificed your *will* upon the altar
as a love offering to Me. Do not hesitate to ask of Me.
Ask, totally trusting My judgment, and *I will deliver* you to
the mission of My choice as an Ambassador to the King. It
may be as near as your neighborhood or as far as encircling
the globe.
Can you abandon yourself without fear or regret to this
service in My name? Your mission journeys may seem like
uncharted waters to you, but O so familiar to Me in the
saving of lost and or troubled souls.
Dear one, I keep the record book of the faithful and that
is all that matters in the eternal scope of things. I reward
deeds well done--- in My Name.

Rest easy---I go before you. Always I prepare the way. I give you to speak words of wisdom, words of encouragement to their fear-ridden hearts.

ABBA   3-1-84

A CALL TO WORSHIP

Psalm 95:6
Come, let us bow down in worship, let us kneel before the Lord our Maker.

Sing out, spare not---beat the drum, and pipe the flute. Bursts of glory ever near. Some do conquer---others fear! Bursts of glory--- a shining light---penetrates the darkness, and sends all evil to flight.

Shimmering strings of silver, splash across the sky; angel trails, My sweet, angel trails of love mark the speckled sky. Bursts of glory ever near---bursts of glories measured light---made to flash and spin about---made to keep man, without a doubt, in turmoil---because man is in fear!

O! How can the savior draw near? Sing out ---spare not---waste not---a call to worship prevents drought.

Bide your time---scan the sky. Look to Him---look to Me, reach out in faith, and trust, O you who are part of My Tree.

Storm clouds will gather----but don't you pout---don't you fret; I have never left My own in debt! Freely take and freely give, step into the water and learn to swim--- Learn to pray and *act on His Word.*

Learn to praise, and be concerned for mankind. Sing a new song, and pipe the flute. Sing a new song---come join the group of over-comers today.

2

Come join the group---it is time to stay within the folds of My protective wings. Bursts of glory shining bright---nectar from heaven the Father's delight.

Beat the drum---beat it well, pipe them aboard and save them from hell; for from your lips to Mine---we say, "salvation;"---we say, "Joy."

We say, "Blessings."---We say, appear to him ---to her in the form of a dove. We say, "Glory" ---"Glory"---raiment (clothing) from above to cover man.

The raiment---His body---His blood poured out for man. Draw from the well that never runs dry. Draw from the well, and wait for His cry, "Be sober, be ready---never run dry; for your lamps are ready, and filled to the brim with the "oil of gladness," free from sin.

Live and reign ----the veil is lifted---torn in two---all because of that *obedient Jew*---which housed My Son; who covenanted to walk in the dust for man!

That He, My Son---might present to Me His bride---the *lovely over-comer* with Him.

Now reign in glory O! Bride and groom, I've given you plenty of room to rule and reign. While on earth ---content you be---to worship the Father---yes Me!

Clear the path until that day, not far from now, you will see constant rays of glory beaming forth, covering all creation in a blanket of love!

We will fellowship together in My theatre above. Draw close in prayer and praise to send forth a heavenly fragrance that fills My chambers with love.

ABBA   6-13-8

A CHRISTIAN MARRIAGE

Hebrews 13:4
    Marriage should be honored by all, and the marriage bed kept pure...

Be very attentive to My Word. A Christian marriage is a Godly state. Remain obedient--- daily, as your schedules allow you both, to read together--- praying and praising Me in the sanctuary of your home.

Do not neglect the time of collective prayer with the joy of your life---your wife, your husband. Be released from all anxiety, confusion, or despair.

Do not listen to the voice from the *dark side;* you can sense him in the changed atmosphere in and about your dwelling place as you begin to commune with Me!

Remain sensitive to My leading; you both are so dearly loved. Stay to the path; (Ps.139:3) (LIV) *O Lord, "You chart the path ahead of me and tell me where to stop and rest."*

Remember: "You are in My care and keeping. Always be in the state of believing faith. Do not fear My corrections...*just follow My directions.*

ABBA   8-14-81

A FEAST OF REMEMBRANCE

1 Cor. 11:24-26
    ...and when He had given thanks, He broke it, and said, "This is my body, which is for you; do this in remembrance of me." In the same way, after supper he took the cup, saying, "This cup is the new covenant in my blood; do this, whenever you

drink it, in remembrance of me." For whenever you eat this bread and drink this cup, you proclaim the Lord's death until he comes.

Take and eat of My body. Take and drink of My blood, freely shed for you. Partake of Me often. Stay close to those who are weak in body, soul and spirit. You be their anchor and strong support. Forgive their short-comings and self-centeredness. Pluck them, through earnest prayer and supplication, from the raging fires of hell itself. Engage them often---teaching, admonishing, praying them towards maturity in Me.

Be that strong servant as you continue to seek out the 'who-so-ever-wills' that do not know much about Me, but are eager to come to know Me.

Take them under your wing, you who are steeped in My word, and gradually bring them toward the path to maturity in Me.

Now---in service to Me put on your *seamless garment* (spiritually) and with the Sword of the Spirit (which is Jesus, the living word) by your side, stand and watch Me work---for, My child, the battle is not yours ---but Mine!

ABBA   4-14-81

A FINISHED WORK YOU WILL BE

Col. 2:10
And you have been given fullness in Christ, who is the head over every power and authority.

Let My promises encourage you as you delve deeper into the study of My Word; *building on that firm foundation,* continuing to insure your growth toward *maturity.*

5

Stay on the alert. Do not allow Satan, the master of deceit, to attack you through guilt. My Spirit will help you to grow in Kingdom living! (Righteousness, peace, and joy in the Holy Spirit.)

Your problems, self made or placed upon you by others or circumstances, are but stepping-stones along the road to what I am completing in you to produce--- *a finished work.*

You must let Me do *it in you.* Allow the Holy Spirit to work from the *inside out,* until the enemy understands that he is no match against My Spirit.

My warrior angels will do the work without your assistance! Your assignment ---pray, and praise Me more until My hoard of angels run the enemy back to the very pits of hell!

My strong right hand of heavenly power and might will bring them under submission.

Keep to the word. That is the fuel that will finish the work toward your maturity. Trust and obey Me, loved one.

Continue to study the word; for from these eternal scriptures will always be your covering in any situation.

Just believe that I AM near, and am closer than a brother; assuring you of victory in all that you attempt to do in My name!

ABBA   8-22-81

A FORK IN THE ROAD

1 Cor. 10:13

No temptation has seized you except what is common to man. And God is faithful; he will not let you be tempted beyond what you can bear. But when you are tempted, he will also provide a way out so that you can stand up under it.

Self---My child, like oil in water, seeks its own level. Temptation is at every turn in the road of life. When you come to a fork in the road---and *certainly you will*, take the high ground. Stand on that sure footing of Christ's redemption on your behalf.

Let it not once be said about you that you took the easy path; the path that leads to the destruction of the high calling I have placed on your life.

Arise to the challenge, trust in your Father who was and is, and ever shall be. Cry out to Me as Satan attempts to sift you like wheat. Jump quickly into the river of life (Ps.46:4-5).

You have been buried in the waters of baptism. Breathe life into the sick and down trodden. Encourage the widow. You know to do right---DO IT!

The true measure of greatness is not measured in mileage. but in the understanding of the tasks set before you---never look back!

ABBA   8-19-81

A FRESH NEW LEVEL OF INTIMACY

Isaiah 26:19
But your dead will live; their bodies will rise. You who dwell in the dust, wake up and shout for joy. Your dew is like the dew of the morning; the earth will give birth to her dead.

Your dead men shall live. Their bodies shall arise. Awake and sing, you that dwell in dust: for your dew is as the dew of herbs, and the earth shall cast out the dead.

I set you on the hill of My convenience; that which oversees your world. The time is very short. The sabers of Satan are rattling, even at this writing to bring on a holocaust that will drive man to despair.

But I will turn his Sabers against the hoards he has hoodwinked through lying words of *future heavenly gain!*

Maggots and worms without end will fill them throughout eternity. O! What an intense white-hot heat will be their lot; one that will never leave them. I---in My justice, will fan the flames!

Speak out as never before---recess is over, dear children; time to pick up your Bibles, and get back to the classroom for intense study of My word.

Sit at the feet of those who have, by their obedience and faithful trust, received and stored up the gift of prophesies; to aid others like yourselves to bring many into the realm of prophesy and declaration---to a waiting world!

Once pronounced, the choice is theirs to accept or deny; grace, peace, and loving success to those who accept the *saying*; for it is from My mouth---through theirs that are speaking!

ABBA   2-12-81

A GREAT DISASTER AHEAD

1 Samuel 17:37

"...the Lord who delivered me from the paw of the lion and the paw of the bear will deliver me

8

from the hand of this Philistine." Saul said to David, "Go, and the Lord be with you."

I tell you that great disasters take place daily upon this earth---*but,* you can come against them.

Pray for the protection from Satan's demonic formed "*radical*" Islamic religion, one that would destroy, if it could, all that My Son came to do: that of bringing every mother's sons and daughters to the foot of the Cross.

Our prayers---along with the prayers of many a *bold intercessor* in My Name---can, and will, turn that evil tide of destruction!

I pose this question: Do you care enough to stand in the gap---fully, with armor in place, and stand along the *last line of defense*-- while I work the work of disposing the demonic forces aimed at My creation, of which you are a part?

Continue to support My right arm of power and might, as I hold it high, administering *Holy Spirit justice!*

Continue to read, praise, and pray. Stand tall, beloveds, stand *tall* in *faith* and *trust* in My Name *alone!*

ABBA

A PLACE FOR SPIRITS TO DWELL

Joshua 24:15

"...if serving the Lord seems undesirable to you, then choose for yourselves this day whom you will serve, whether the gods your forefathers served beyond the River, or the gods of the Amorites, in whose land you are living. But as for me and my household, we will serve the LORD."

What price war---what price peace? Strangers in foreign lands---it was ever so. Man in himself is a hollow shell---a place for spirits to dwell---for good or for evil--- *which will it be?*

Was My Name ever taught while on some mother's knee? Strangers in paradise, My Name newly formed on their lips. Strangers in paradise---but *your prayers* have brought them in.

Dearly beloved---you who are anchored in the Word pray for the "Peace of Jerusalem"---pray, and give forth My word. Set your sights on the task ahead. Great unrest will rule *all lands.*

Notice how the shaking has begun. Sit back with the word in hand---sit back and watch Me work! Offer that cup of *'cool clear water.'* Take them by the hand---I soon send you to another land or place. There I expect you to grow and seek out the lost and infirm.

Freely open your hand---for with the measure you give--- a double portion for you is at hand! Be on the alert--- screen every word. Notice the people who are getting out of control. In quietness, and assurance, be their guide to the light of the Savior of their souls. No man is perfect, this I know, but a vessel *broken in My Name*, becomes free to come and go! Go when the light is given.

My way and path will be made clear. Do not move --- do not budge, until My circumstances appear, then freely go to another land (or place). A place that I have prepared---one that can show the love I have for your fellow man.

ABBA   2-3-91

A PLACE OF REST

Rev. 14:13

10

Then I heard a voice from heaven say, "Write: Blessed are the dead who die in the Lord from now on." "Yes," says the Spirit, "they will rest from their labor, for their deeds will follow them."

There is a plane---a higher plane---where His own must walk. There is a plane where God resides! In the Holiness of God His meadows are clear, flawless and true. The grass so green; here they stop, and rest surrounded by the early dew.

The light---a Hazel blue, purifies each saint who passes through. To those that abide, and reach the plane---I say, "Lay down your cross and be still."

Gleaming angels' wings protect your paths, allowing your purposes to be fulfilled. Pause and refresh yourself from the well of life. Let your sinews and mind be renewed.

There is a plane ---a lower plane, where God's children live and work---a plane worn and so rough shod, that cockle burrs are present and would snare and snag God's elect.

Here the cross must be applied. Here God's own must cease and rest. Here too your angels preen themselves and measure the ominous skies.

There strength abides as we pray and lift our spirits heavenward. All praise to Him, who builds and prepares His saints—even while it is still day. We must work --- lifting up the cross to him and to her who is mired in the avalanche of time. Bring them to the higher plane---where they can live and abide!

ABBA

A REED SHAKEN BY THE WIND

Mt. 11:7

As John's disciples were leaving, Jesus began to speak to the crowd about John: "What did you go out into the desert to see? A reed swayed by the wind?"

What did you come to see? Rich men parading their expensive clothing at their elite affairs or did you through hail and snow brave the elements to hear one of My prophets laud and praise My name?

Do not be shaken by temporary setbacks, large or small; for I Am Almighty God who, by My mouth---brought forth billions upon billions of Galaxies for you to marvel at My Greatness!

You can know without a shadow of doubt---that I AM able to satisfy all your present and future needs on planet earth, and to bring you safely to My bosom at life's end on earth...to My kingdom to explore all of My creations.

I AM beyond your comprehension now in your limited earthly body. But O! The grandeur that lies before you when I bring you to your eternal home to experience; for all eternity---without restraints, to view and experience: Kingdom Living of righteousness, peace and joy in the Holy Spirit.

I will feed you with joy and clarity, sharing the sights of the universe itself! You will join the heavenly angels in song and worship, singing My praises as I gather you all into My bosom of love!

I admonish you now beloved—Be patient---with perseverance and persistence, to finish the tasks, reaching out to common man who have never heard My name: "Jesus." Bring them into My care and keeping!

Give Me all of yourself; to be used with the gifts I have created in you---in service to Me!

ABBA   11-25-09

A WORD FOR THOSE IN HIGH OFFICE

Psalm 2:2
The kings of the earth take their stand and the rulers gather together against the Lord and against his Anointed One. "Let us break their chains," they say, "and throw off their fetters."

I say a word to---those in high office, the so-called *royally treated ones*---even the Christian elite,   "Rely on the *ultimate King*, the very King of Glory, before attempting to make any decisions which affect others---and even *nations*.

Your Master—He is saying, "Your work has just begun; follow My leading."

Stay free. There are others to be won; but the cares of this world have bogged them down, and blinded they are. They are Mine, and I give them no rest . . . no peace . . . until they rest in Me.

Obey the constitution set down by those whom I chose long ago to faithfully construct, and preserve.

Be not high-minded, putting yourself above those you were called to protect. Remember I, the King of Glory, humbled Myself before My disciples, girded Myself and washed their feet. Can you (in spirit) do less?

A word of warning: Treat your countrymen with humble respect, or I will snatch your candle from its lamp stand, and leave you!

Live a life of obedience to My headship, (leadership) and be open to serve your fellow man.

ABBA   6-7-81

A WORD OF CORRECTION

Proverbs 23:13
   Withhold not correction from the child: for if you
beat him with the rod, he shall not die.

I command you to take your hands off close loved ones.
Don't try to force My hand for their well-being; I have told
you before about this!
   I know your heart---but you must *wait* on My timing in
all things; not just health needs! You know to do right---do
it!
   Trust me *O man of My heart; My timing is* perfect, and
is multi tasked---*Selah* (*Pause and think about this*).
   Your lives, at times, when "troubled waters" envelope
you, affects many lives of those near and far---at the same
time!
   Therefore ---I continue to guide you and your beloveds,
and all who put their trust in Me. Take heart---I AM your
faithful Father---*I slumber not!* O! My child ---the things I
have in store for you---and all those who put their trust in
Me   Know that you are *already* living in eternity---Is that
too hard for you to understand?

ABBA

A WORD OF ENCOURAGEMENT

1 Cor. 15:58
   Therefore, my dear brothers, stand firm. Let
nothing move you. Always give yourselves fully to
the work of the Lord, because you know that your
labor in the Lord is not in vain.

14

Like the man blind from birth who was brought forth seeing---all for the glory of God, so shall you burst forth into newness of life for all to see as My steadfast witnesses. (Jn. 9:1-7)

Stand tall, dress yourselves in your finest. Let not the world see your spiritual fast as you struggle for that confused one's eternal salvation.

Do not fret, do not stew, tomorrow is another day for glorious victory. Not a hair on your head, not a stitch of your clothes will be lost in this battle for the soul of man, woman, or child. Be courageous---steady . . . My storehouse is full, and your portion is being emitted as needed. I do not lie as man---but am true to My promises— Man need not attempt to defend My honor.

Your work is to stand beside Me dressed in your battle gear with the *Sword of the Spirit* by your side.

Sing a song of victory as you watch Me work on your behalf!

ABBA   3-6-81

ALL HAVE GONE ASTRAY

Psalm 14:3

All have turned aside, they have together become corrupt; there is no one who does good, not even one.

How strong the currents of habit---How strong is the tug of war? "How deeply imbedded are the sins of your past. No man dare laugh you to scorn."

All we, ---like sheep have gone astray. All we like sheep are borne by the winds of desire; borne by the seeds of despair.

15

Fear not little flock---fear not. I have come to seek and to save. Cry out, O wild one, cry out, far into the night; for My sheep know Me---and My name.

O! Yes---I was there when you had need of repair, but you would not admit your wrongs or yield for repair! You practiced in your heart to rebel.

You practiced to manipulate mankind in your *own small way*. Ultimate defeat--- spurred you on--- even when you knew better---*habit has its hold!*

Man---made in My image, struggles on--- seeking peace and balance to his life. Man in his struggle---falls into furrows deeply grooved by life. Strong currents of habit continue to hang on!

"Must I ever give ground to My habit and sin--- O Lord, and is there *any end* to this tug of war? When does victory begin"?

It begins O child of God---when you realize that the battle is not yours---but Mine.

I have called you to a life free from despair. I have called you to a life in Me. Now let go in your body, soul and spirit, and follow Me.

Give unto others as I have given to you. Let your desire be to serve and rescue man. Overpower that which is in you that would live in discontent.

Yes, you in the flesh are imperfect, O man. Yes, you in the flesh are striving on---regardless of cost to yourself and family!

Remember the former days when your battles were won. Come now---kneel before Me and pray. Let your praises fill the sanctuary of your heart. Let your spiritual eyes be full.

Yes, My glory is revealed in prayer and praise. Take the time to read My Word---It will keep you straight along the path of righteousness, peace, and joy in the Holy Spirit.

O weep not, O man born from *perfect* dust. I have freed you from all sin. Now---in the power of My Name---walk in My light---the very light of Jesus--- My beloved Son!

ABBA   6-20-90

ARE YOU CARRYING OLD BAGGAGE

John 8:36
   So if the son sets you free, you will be free
indeed.

Do have hidden chambers in your soul where you keep your old sinful baggage, unable to die to your own unregenerate past?

Old sins are so deeply engrained that you allow them to come forth in an unguarded moment of built in rage or even illicit passions that you are still dealing with.

Dearest child---find a quiet time of self-examination, guided by My Holy Spirit. If you truly want to be made free
and serve Me all the remaining days of your life, make the decision today to become free of this world's entanglements and old temptations.

I will lift you up *above the fray*; protecting you from the onslaughts of satanic suggestions. I came to earth to lead you out of turmoil and self-aggrandizement, open to a life free from Satan's lies and distractions.

We are at war, loved one, for the prince of this world has declared it! He tested Me in the wilderness and after forty days and forty nights said, "If You are the Son of God, command that these stones become bread."

17

I responded, "It is written, 'Man shall not live on bread alone---but on every word that proceeds out of the mouth of God'. "

You too must memorize this passage, and when temptation rears its ugly head---reply to his suggestions in the *negative* and you will defeat his efforts to bring you into his fold. You whom God has freed to live a consecrated life dedicated to My will!

Do this with your hidden baggage: Bring them back to your recollection---then once and for all *repent* of their nagging presence and be free from their hold on your life!

Now---repentant one---rally to the *call* I have placed on your life, and be free to serve Me and mankind in *newness of life* free from the baggage that so totally plagued you in your battle for the souls of Man!

For the battle is not yours but Mine. Stand now and watch Me keep you free in Me, as you minister in My name!

ABBA 9-27-09

ARE YOU A LIGHT TO THE BLIND

Romans 2:19
...If you are convinced that you are a guide for the blind, a light for those who are in the dark...

Are you a light to the blind? Or do you hide your light under a bushel? Do you "study to show yourself approved unto God"? Or do the *daily cares of this world* keep you from serving the father---with all that He made you to be?

To you who have stayed connected with Me these many years---as you count years, I say, "Well done good and faithful servant."

You have, like Saint Paul, let this world, and all its *tinsel*, not have any hold on you. You do need to spend more time in the word---exploring more of the hidden and fenced in things that I have for you to learn.

It does please Me that you find many *Ramah* words---which I use for the titles of new messages I bring to your heart of hearts---for your care and keeping! [*Those words that the Lord brings to your attention, that seem to jump off the pages to your heart.]

These are messages that the who-so-ever-wills of this world can latch on to and know they come from My heart to your heart as you pick up your pen to write them down. I bless you for that!

ABBA   7-31-09

O! Lord---it is an honor that you have bestowed upon your servant: that the Creator of this world, and Creator of all the Galaxies in the expanding universes would speak to His creation.

Words cannot express my feelings, nor describe the excitement I feel as You begin to speak to me. I am in awe of my father God!

I will continue to obey you all the days that you have left for me on this earth, living a life that is pleasing to You---and to my family and friends alike!

It is truly an honor to be found faithful in the administration of distributing your Word in this world!

ARE YOU LISTENING

John 6:60
On hearing it, many of his disciples said, "This is a hard teaching. Who can accept it?"

I will not always strive with man. The fullness of time is fast approaching. All who hear My voice will come in and sup with Me, and I with them. I tell you this so that you will not grow weary when I send you in after them with My help! (Rev. 3:20) "Behold, I stand at the door and knock: if any man hear my voice and open the door, I will come in to him and will eat with him and he with Me."

Throw them, that are drowning, the rope of salvation. Hurdle the turbulent waters. Shore-up the walls. I AM taking you into a wide world of service---in prayer and in spirit---in actuality. You have full and complete coverage surrounded by your warrior angels:---*flames of fire* are burning a trail of fire that Satan and his dark ones cannot put out.

Trust not your own earthly abilities to take on the enemy by yourself, for he is a formidable foe. Prepare to do battle through your believing prayers and praises; then watch how I work things out in your behalf.

I AM never late nor early but you can count on it---I *AM always on time.*

Strive for the high ground; stretch your potential...release the gifts I have blessed you with. Count the 'shepherds'---resting on the park benches of life, watching endless souls heading for the brink...it shall not be so with you! Stand in the gap---ward them off, loved ones.

ABBA   5-24-81

20

ARE YOU STILL FIGHTING LOST CAUSES

Phil. 3:7-8
But whatever was to my profit I now consider
loss for the sake of Christ. What is more, I consider
everything a loss compared to the surpassing
greatness of knowing Christ Jesus my Lord, for
whose sake I have lost all things. I consider them
rubbish, that I may gain Christ.

Don't fight lost causes---consign them to the rubbish heap
and walk on in *newness of life* in Me. When you sought
My guidance on your behalf, I repeatedly declared these
causes *not winnable.*

Why do you insist on going it *on your own?* If you will
look closely at your decisions---you will see *total pride*
raising its ugly head right before your eyes!

There is no shame in stopping a cause that to you seems
winnable. I have the advantage of being *outside of time*; I
can see the beginning from the end.

Stop any action on your part to continue pursuing that
lost cause. Rather, turn your energies in another direction
as I guide your efforts. Be absorbed in My fight for
common man, the end of which will bring joy to My heart!

Get engaged in helping the poor, the lame, and the
outcasts of this world---through no fault of their own. They
want love and caring for all their needs. Let them know that
they are not rejected, worthless or degraded persons, but a
very dear part of your crumbling world in this *powder keg*
atmosphere of worldly unrest.

With Satan and his demons let loose worldwide with
satanic plans to bring their agenda to the forefront, know
beyond a doubt that your world is at war.

Lucifer, who led the revolt of the angels before his fall,
is making his strongest effort in these last days to disrupt,

maim, and kill all who refuse to follow his ways; therefore stay on the alert, and stay very close to My Spirit--- who will guide you into all truth and keep you safe from his evil ways.

Soon, O! So very soon I will stop his madness and confine him to the fiery pits of hell along with his hoards of demons!

ABBA   9-28-09

BABES IN CHRIST

1 Cor. 2:2
    For I resolved to know nothing while I was with you except Jesus Christ and him crucified

Babes in Christ on milk with little or no understanding of the deeper things of God! Babes in Christ, insisting on staying on a milk diet, fearful of what the Lord may have to say about their present journey--- through their walk on earth!

Fearful of what lies ahead of them, day by day, they are moved by My Spirit to start a new life with Me, and tired of the fantasies and short comings in their present walk.

They have chosen to enter the fellowship of believers--- taking on the responsibilities of studying My word.

To those who have come to Me in obedience to My Spirit, ----driven, if you will, to find out more of the Lord God Almighty, with a hunger to know My Son--- I say, "Welcome to My everlasting kingdom!"

Dearest, honest seeker, know that My Spirit abides in you---in your inner man; for you, My child, are a reflection of the Trinity: body----soul---and spirit, a triune being. We in heaven and earth are known as Father, Son and Holy

Spirit---balancing the equation; for I made all things to be in balance---in heaven and on earth!

My Spirit has come to reside in your bodily frame, to lead and guide you on this earthly testing ground---where I will teach you heavenly things--- things that you have had, or will have---hardships of every kind to prepare you for service to the who-so-ever-wills that I will send across your path, and to bring you through a child-like faith, and on into a maturing faith in Me.

Know that winds---good and bad experiences---will come along teaching you to become an experienced warrior in My army---here on earth!

My Spirit will take you---step by step through My love letter (Bible) to you. O! The joy that awaits you as you begin to understand My messages of *wisdom* and *comfort* and yes---*correction* that will take you along the road toward maturity---with a burning love for Me---your maker and constant companion.

I caution you to walk in the light with Jesus in every way!

ABBA   1-13-09

BE IMITATORS OF ME

1 Cor. 11:1
Follow my example as I follow the example of Christ.

Can you look into your heart of hearts, and from the depths of your inner man---make the same claim? The majority of My followers are so involved in their day-to-day lives that, outside of *lip service,* in most churches today they worship by rote and do not walk in My paths of righteousness, peace, and joy in the Holy Spirit.

Yet there are many on-fire churches that have begun to stir the lives of our young adults who take-up the very front rows of these churches that have sprung up, totally giving up their lives of comfort and ease, taking their turn on the mission fields where Christianity is not prevalent.

They have heard the cry of young pastors and have resounded with an affirmative: "Yes! I will go---send me."

The young college age adults are taking their relationships with serious commitments, as young couples, not rushing into a hasty marriage, but are getting well grounded in the faith and trust in Me as their highest priority as I mold them into the likeness of My Son's passion to reach the unsaved of the world. And they are seriously committing their lives to go into "all the world" as never before since Christ walked the paths of this world gathering the who-so-ever-wills unto the righteous paths, seeking—always seeking the *halt, lame and blind.*

To all you young adults who have truly given your care and keeping into My hands: I salute you---O bearers of My Name!

Keep soaking in the word and give yourselves over to going deeper into My messages to gather a lost multitude!

Use your youthful talents and energy to complete the call I have placed on your lives.

ABBA   10-28-09

BE STILL MY HEART

Psalms 138:7

Though I walk in the midst of trouble, you preserve my life; you stretch out your hand against

24

the anger of my foes, with your right hand you save me. The LORD will fulfill his purpose for me; your love, O LORD, endures forever—do not abandon the works of your hands.

What passion confounds the hearts and minds of man? What passion in the flesh---blinds My disciples' foot steps? What passion birthed from the inner man, tied as one with My Spirit, clears the path, and reveals My mind in the things of man---and his daily walk?

Where but in the silence of this present hour can you draw away from your daily tasks and listen---in silence, to My heartbeat---*It beats, dear one, for you.*

My eyes roam the world in search of those who will obediently follow My leading---even to the point of bleeding for a lost and degenerate world!

Think it not strange---this thing that has come upon you. Experience My Son even in His rejection. Who, more than He, was misunderstood---even to the final shedding of His blood.

Can you do less---you who have thrown your lot in with Him? For like as a mother hen gives warmth and comfort to her young chicks---so, I through Him give you comfort in this your hour of pain!

Get through your period of grieving, and press on along that rugged path. There is much work to do, and a heavy burden lies along that path, for *man is losing his way.*

Your task, "Make disciples for Me." Quicken your step now, for I alone---carry the *load!*

ABBA

BELIEVING PRAYER

James 5:16
Confess your sins to each other and pray for each other so that you may be healed. The prayer of a righteous man is powerful and effective.

Testify to the glow of the resurrection power within you.

Continue to pray into existence 'things' nurtured, and conceived by prayer. *Believing prayer* brings you and others like you to replenish the land---strengthened by My hand!

Many come ---many look---so few 'take' of the wine whose grapes have been sacrificed to provide nourishment for the soul and sweet communion with My Spirit! Your task is to uphold the weak and encourage the strong. Defeat the enemy wherever you find him. Be instant in prayer---slow to anger---quick to forgive. Forgive man and encourage him to reach greater heights in Me

ABBA

BRICK UPON BRICK-STONE UPON STONE

Isaiah 61:4
They will rebuild the ancient ruins and restore the places long devastated; they will renew the ruined cities that have been devastated for generations.

Flush the sewers---clear the channels and stand back as you prepare to rebuild.

O! Repairer of the breach---you who are willing to *stand in the gap,* I salute you---I greet you---I bless you with a Holy kiss.

My treasure house is full and I am about to pay. I have heard your petitions---and so now I can act on them; I have heard your decisions, but they still lack the fuller commissions.

But do not fret---they don't lack zeal--- even gaining an inch at a time, *never look back.* Brick upon brick---stone upon upon stone---each time you experience a success---the natural expansion of My power *through you* will save many from storm-filled seas.

Just now beloved---ponder and dream. See each picture of the finished work up ahead. Bring yourself to prayer and praise. Speak the Word clearly and define each base (subject at hand).

Wield your mighty hand with clear-cut instructions--- always from Me! Sharpen your inner man. Ponder and praise My Name and you, My children, will see that it is I---It is Me---that prepares your way.

What a joy---what a blessing you are to Me. Ride the trade winds---ride them for Me. Your heavenly business: the in-gathering of the who-so-ever wills. Bring them--- bring them to My Throne room---and I will give them *rest.*

ABBA   1-31-83

THE BRIGHTNESS OF HIS GLORY
(His Attributes)

Ex.24:16-17

"...and the glory of the LORD settled on Mount Sinai. ...To the Israelites the glory of the LORD

27

looked like a consuming fire on top of the mountain.

Would you see the brightness of My Glory? Would you see Me in *all My Glory*? Not so My beloved…not on this side of the Vail; but see Me in your spirit just now.

Try as you might, the physical eye would be blinded by even a lesser light; *you call it the Sun*. How much more the *intensity of* My burning energy; My white hot heat.

Man pales, and is consumed within his breast, at My majesty. Can you see who is pure, who is clean; who rides upon the crest of love enduring earth's tattered garments of pain and shame?

You were created to share My *light* made in My image, a pure delight to Me, an aroma of heavenly perfume---but man gave it all away for a *mess of pottage*…threw away his right to see Me as I really am!

Listen to this message of hope…listen to me please!

Want to experience light *on the way*? Want to experience Me Now? Then set yourself apart for Me; then view My written Word

Study it without ceasing; never let a day go by without taking the time to indulge yourself in the Word.

How your hearts will burn within as you muse and ponder the light. See Me reflected in each page you turn! Feel My gentle touch of love caress your spirit, give you peace, and fill your heart with joy…cleansing your hearts!

Free My hands to do the work through you, as they are freed-up in prayer. Let your light shine before man [Mt. 5:14]. Be obedient to My commands of love so dearly won for all!

Stagger not at the work ahead.

We, together, conquer one day at a time. You are Mine you know; even from head to toe! I send you out in *a flame of fire* that none can see...but *all* will feel *our heat*...you and I combined... to shine heaven's light along the path to My Heavenly home.

ABBA   10-3-08

BRING COMFORT AND JOY

Psalm 119:28-29
My soul is weary with sorrow; strengthen me according to your word. Keep me from deceitful ways. Be gracious to me though your law.

O! Father---as I reflect on your goodness this early morn, I am reminded of the day that You, in Your wisdom, put me *on the world's shelf,* as I walked the streets discouraged and in despair as a teenager---pondering life's *meaning.*

You brought me, at nineteen, through World War II, into Your world of safety, purpose, and direction. Your timing allowed me to look to you for hope and the reason for my very existence.

You taught me to *hunger and thirst* after You, as I picked up Your word (Bible), and started on the path of getting to *know* You.

You saved me at the age of twenty-four---by giving me the love of my life, which lasted fifty seven years, before you brought her to Your kingdom!

Her obedience in putting up with my *deep-seated immaturity in those early days of our marriage* kept me close to You all these many years.   She was truly a wonderful spirit-filled lady---a loving companion with the patience of Job, and persistence.

We started reading and studying Your word together every morning---and then we offered You our collective prayers, petitions, and praises.

It is a pleasure to serve You in the fight for common man; You sent across our path people to teach. With Your guidance and help we nurtured them, with encouragement, to follow Your Son, Jesus.

O! My child---you served Me well, and your life together was an inspiration to all whom I led to cross your path!

Now that your loved one is home with Me, you remain steady, delving deeper into My word to find the fenced in and hidden things in My field, the pearl of great price. You found that pearl---Jesus (Mt. 13:46).

You have been collecting all the messages, (since 1980), that I have given you, and still do, to pick-up your pen and write them in a book for the world to read.

I know that you miss her physical presence, after being together these many years; she is with Me, experiencing kingdom living!

She sees Me In all of My glory, and I see her in all of her glory, experiencing all of My universe, along with family and friends who had gone on before her.

What joy will fill her heart, waiting for you that day, after your work for Me is done on this earth. I will greet your homecoming, saying, "Well done good and faithful servant ---enter into the house of your Lord!"

ABBA   7-27-09

BURST FORTH O SUN

Jeremiah 5:24

They do not say to themselves, Let us fear the LORD our God, who gives fall and spring rains in season, who assures us of the regular weeks of harvest.

Burst forth, O Sun---cover all things under your wing---shadows of doubt and fear---shadows of things to come --- always draw near.

Why is it, O Sun, that things under the earth have the potential to *appear* from your mighty light coupled with *rain*.

The mighty struggle for life begins, and then, in time---rears its head, as like a plant pushing its way through its opposition until---bathed in your warming light---and heaven-sent rain, its very life begins, and tall and straight it grows---*for a season.*

Burst forth O Son---cover all things with your sting. Send forth conviction into their doubting, *fear-ridden hearts.*

Let mankind cry out, hear them shout, "Do it unto me---in love! Spread your wings, O Dove, and light on me.
Fill my heart and direct my way, for Your paths for me are clear!

You took my place---O Lamb of God---You took my place so I could see. You are the "Former and Latter Rain."
You---You are the one that everyone should acclaim.

For though I lie buried in a sea of sin---only the Savior has the key to come in and fill my heart with love. You, only You, can say, "Peace be still---I calm the waters just now."

You, only You, have the power to till the soil of my heart---and prepare it well. Ready for the seeds of plenty---seeds of grace, seeds of love for man---to be turned into the newly plowed soil of man---set free by your *Latter rain.*

Burst forth, O Son, and be ready when man rebels. He was given dominion over all things---in a day---He was given dominion as he heard Me say, "Till the soil, and name the flocks. Take dominion ---record the shocks.

For into your hands this day---have I put you in charge of all things here on earth. 'Stay the course'---guard the sheep and record the events that led even to My feet.

For at the cross---I paid it all for man, woman and child!"

ABBA

CALLED TO DO HIS WILL

John 4:34
"My food," said Jesus, "is to do the will of him who sent me and to finish his work."

My *will* is for you to do as did My Son, finish the work that I have sent you to do!

Many are called, but few are chosen. *(Mt. 20:16) I know who are mine, and when given by My Spirit a call to go here or there, My "called-out ones" will respond, first counting the cost, then by reporting for duty a*s the Holy Spirit directs! Seeking the troubled hearts with no self*-esteem. Helping the blind *to see* and read *My word;* also aiding the undernourished poor of this world.

Yes, also some unfortunate ones who will become awakened to life eternal by you, dearest child. ---Open the scriptures to their waiting ears of a 'life in My Son' and *set them free from sin and death.*

Hear the story of Mephibosheth of old, crippled at birth, by a servant who dropped him, while carrying him in her arms.

He was invited by King David to eat at his table, the only surviving son of King Saul. King David gave him all of Saul's wealth accumulated during his lifetime! (2 Sam. 21:7-8)

Learn this lesson My child: These are the blessings that are given My own.... the right to witness God's grace and provision to those who are called to serve man for Me, attesting to the love of My Son Jesus; and My open hand, giving them access to the greatest treasure of all: to see Me face to face and to enjoy kingdom living: righteousness, peace, and joy in the Holy Spirit.

ABBA   8-3-09

CALM BE STILL

Ps. 46:10
Be still, and know that I am God; I will be exalted among the nations, I will be exalted in the earth.

I AM He El Shaddai . . . I AM He who formed the language of love through the Word made flesh---He who suffered unspeakable injustices---He who withstood the evil one---He who is "My bright and Morning star." (Rev. 22:16) You who bear His name---can you do less?
I AM Almighty God, and need no defense.
O that finite man would, by My Spirit, put his trust in Me— for just as I formed man from the pure dust of the earth I continued to give man new birth, new freedom, a changed life as he accepts the forgiveness of sin in his or her life through what My Son did on the cross.
Now as you grow in grace and maturity---be at peace--- be at rest in your distress. I AM your fortress and you are bound with My thongs of love!

ABBA   2-12-03

CAST YOUR BREAD UPON THE WATER

John 21:6

He said, "Throw your net on the right side of the boat and you will find some." When they did, they were unable to haul the net in because of the large number of fish.

I love---care---and nurture you as a loving parent that I AM. I birthed you into this world of trials and suffering but, dearly beloveds, for the world's *greater good!*

You have ---"cast your bread upon the waters. *(Eccles. 11:1) Now watch it as I receive it as food for My Being!

Know you this---I AM in charge of all that is on your *'platter'* this day; none of it will sour or be lost!

For they---your opposition, do not realize what is sent your way to defeat you will turn back to them. Consider Mordecai and his enemy Haman who ordered gallows to be built thinking to destroy Mordecai....only to perish on it himself.

Victory on your behalf is assured---a gift---if you will consistently move toward more growth in *Kingdom living,* toward *patience* and *endurance.*

Stand now in your protective armor while I reduce their battle thrusts to a position of complete defeat!

ABBA   7-21-83

CASUAL ACQUAINTANCE

Jer. 29:13

You will seek Me and find Me when you seek me with all your heart.

What degree of thought do you give me? Do you send a quick prayer and hope I hear and honor it? I AM your loving Father God who has given you so many deeds of grace that you take for granted things I have implanted, fixed firmly, in your very being!

I have been watching out for all of My creation since the beginning of time. Man has--- with his modern inventions, some for good and some that have worn the earth into a state of shock ---tainted the air you breath with contaminates to the point of helping to destroy your very being.

Come to the place of light and life and I will show you the fenced in things and the hidden things---all found in My guarded messages of love (Bible)---things for health and welfare, directions for your time on this planet---and, so much more.

Won't you give Me your *will?* I will take you on a glorious adventure all the days of your life. I will satisfy all your needs---but perhaps not all your wants. Your wants are gifted to you as I see fit. Stop from your busy day and look about you. All that you have for your enjoyment I have created.

As you get to know Me, through the written word, you too will have a trusting faith in Me, along with others who have cast their eyes on My willing, tireless servants, who have looked upon those they see and talk to, who are without hope or direction.

Get to know these tireless servants through your church but mainly through small groups of believers who meet in households, bonding with and serving each other according to their needs. Some of their needs are ones of desperation!

O! Come to the *water of life* and experience My love poured out---in your behalf!

ABBA   8-21-09

CHANGED LIVES PROVE MINISTRY

2 Cor. 3:3
You show that you are a letter from Christ, the
result of our ministry, written not with ink but with
the Spirit of the living God, not on tablets of stone
but on tablets of human hearts.

*Thank you Lord for redeeming the time that the
cankerworms have eaten, for I was born in sin (original
sin). My body and spirit were in great conflict. I wanted to
serve you but felt myself to be a prisoner of my own body,
my natural inclinations doing battle with my spirit. (Rom
7:24)*

*But you knew me from my birth and set me on the shelf
for a spell. I was wandering about in utter confusion and
despair; you allowed me to fail time after time, but in my
inner man, was that desire to succeed in all that I attempted
to do, to always finish what I started. And after my
conversion to the Lord Jesus Christ, You ---without my
awareness, charted the paths before me, and told me where
to stop and rest! (Ps. 139:3).*

*Driven by hungering and thirsting to know You better, I
gave my life over to You to do with it as You will!*

Yes---My child---I knew you would come off the shelf
and become a minister for Me, dedicating your life to My
care and keeping!

*O! Lord this world, with all its trinkets and pleasures,
has no hold on me. I rededicate all that you have made me
to be through suffering, (physically and mentally). You
allowed me to go through difficulties, honing my life to
serve you all the rest of my days, for I know the reality of
Your presence!*

My child, continue to reach the world through the messages that I have called you to write. I will send, through your obedience, <u>His Word From Above</u> to reach a multitude of readers in your lifetime---so you can enjoy the fruits of your labor---O! Faithful one.

ABBA   7-22-09

CLEANSE YOUR TEMPLE

Ps. 19:12-13
> Who can discern his errors? Forgive my hidden faults. Keep your servant also from willful sins; may they not rule over me. Then will I be blameless, innocent of great transgression.

Child of My heart, there are many compartments to keep your hidden secrets in; and as you walk through life, you begin to fill these compartments of willful sin and quickly forget about them instead of dealing with them while they are still fresh on your conscious mind!

They soon become rancid without the light of My forgiveness; some have been there for years, and you have lost the sensitivity to open those compartments and deal with them through *obedience* and repentance!

So your temple (body) remains unclean and open to the enemy for further attacks, keeping you from all that you can be--- in service to Me!

Quiet yourself just now and seek My face; ask Me to open those compartments---one at a time; I promise you, loved one, that I will, through the Holy Spirit, cleanse them---one at a time! This is why I said to you over and over through these many messages, as I quickened My scribe to listen for words from My throne of Grace and put his pen to paper for your enlightenment: My promises are true but conditional on obedience and a lifestyle of repentance to keep you from storing up all sins that have accumulated---large or small.

Get alone now with the Word, and as you read and pray, using My name, I will make you to be clean indeed!

ABBA   11-22-09

COME SIT WITH ME

Eph. 2:6
And God raised us up with Christ and seated us with him in the heavenly realms in Christ Jesus..."

Come sit with Me in the heavenly realm free from all the world's cares! Remember loved one---when you take up your cross, take up your sword (Eph. 6:17) "The sword of the Spirit---which is *the word of God.*" And follow Me wherever I lead you. Speak the word to the who-so-ever-wills, those who are seeking to know Me.

Bring them out of darkness into the *light of My Word* (Jesus). Never, never look back, for the success of your efforts comes from *looking ahead* to the *hills of opportunity* to give out and speak My word to the who-so-ever wills.

I created you to be a servant and a town crier without charge. I long to give---out of the *abundance* of My heart---gifts that you thought would not come to you: things that to you and others were thrown away.

I have worked *through man* to give you back what you thought was *lost forever.* Your angels are always on the lookout for you, through others, working to increase your faith and trust in Me. Remember: "My hand is not short that it cannot save." (Isa. 59:1)

Out of what seemed like a great loss I resurrected a gift to serve you in your desperate time of need ---for a season. A great lesson to your children---that I reward those who constantly think about Me, as do you My beloved child, continually praying and praising ---in faith---believing that I am *always on time* to answer your obedient requests!

This *resurrected gift* will teach a great lesson to your children---that I AM always near---working through My angelic beings to watch over you and yours---*in all ways!*

ABBA   7-1-09

COME WALK WITH ME TODAY

Hebrews 1:9
"You have loved righteousness and hated wickedness; therefore God, your God, has set you above your companions by anointing you with the oil of joy."

We will travel the highways and the byways together looking for man---made in My image---lost and without a compass, rudderless—not knowing that, "I AM the way, the truth and the life."

O! Degenerate man (who would stop at nothing to get satisfaction) you have lost your way. In the fields of plenty, yet you do not stop and eat of the fruit of the vine that only I can give you—without cost!

But you will not even stop and take a drink of *cool clear water* to replenish yourself---in your haste to find the *path* that would lead you to My resting place!

For your *pride* will not allow you to stop and ask a brother or sister the way to My house of worship!

What drives you, O man, as you look for the, water of life? You will not humble yourself to come to Me for rest from the trials and tribulations that challenge you each waking day!

So you walk on---busying yourself with *earthly trinkets* and earthly pleasures that have no *eternal value.*

If you seek Me with all your heart, you will find that I AM but a step away. I touch your eyes just now with water mixed with My saliva---that you may see that I am here beside you, tugging at your heart.

O! Man scurrying about with no clear direction open your eyes---and you will see the path that leads to *life everlasting.* It is the highway—washed clean with My blood that will set you free to become all that I made you to be, a royal son or daughter of the King.

Come back to Me and be washed and made clean; then come and sit at My royal table. You will hear Me say, "Take and eat from my larder (pantry) and receive everlasting life."

Then ---O son and daughter---put on your seamless garment and we together will hunt and find other brothers or sisters who have lost their way, bringing them to My table of grace to rest from their travels; for this world is not their home, and the new energy they feel in their inner man is the compass that will lead them safely to My place of rest from all their labors!

We will search the highways and the byways for degenerate men and save them from themselves, helping them to find the *oil of gladness,* finding their way to their heavenly home; for I have anointed you with the *oil of gladness.*

What joy there will be in heaven, as we together find other souls who have lost their way and bring them back to the Father of light.

ABBA   8-14-09

COMING INTO THE LIGHT

Matthew 5:16
Let your light shine before men, that they may see your good deeds, and praise your Father in heaven.

You have come into the light of My love and understanding. I bless you for your courage along with others who freely, in faith, seek My Face.

I bless you for standing tall ---hungering for the truth of the ages: yes, the persons of the trinity---Father, Son, and Holy Spirit.

In quietness ---come and drink of the purest waters, with trust and obedience, learning more and more of Me --- But with a price: dying to self and *what ifs*. I guide you daily through your ministering angels, kept and guarded by My strong right hand of power unknown to the unconverted; for you walk not alone!

Wait on My leading; I will unfold---through undeniable circumstances ---the paths you are to follow.

Fear not, little children of My Heart, ---Fear not!

ABBA

CONTINUE TO MEET THE CHALLENGES

Psalm 17:8
Keep me as the apple of your eye; hide me in the shadow of Your wings.

Deut. 33:12
The Lord shall cover him all the day long, and he shall dwell between his shoulders.

Continue to meet the challenges of the day; for I AM not only in you, by My Spirit, but with you ---setting about a hedge of protection, covering you from all the attacks of the enemy ---as you walk in service to Me, O faithful follower of the Way, in the tasks I have assigned to you.

Know that your *gifts* of love, praise, and worship are *acceptable* in My sight!

ABBA

CROOKED PATHS MADE STRAIGHT

Hebrews 12:13
And make level paths for your feet, so that the lame may not be disabled, but rather healed.

I saw what seemed like a wrinkled worm and a man was walking on top of it---The worm proved to be man's pathway through life---and as he reads, praises, and prays---each segment of the wrinkle (or rough spot) becomes smooth and flat. W.G.M.

How flat and smooth, as I ponder, praise and pray! Joy is mine and the Savior divine and then I hit a snag, running into another ripple, another wave---another valley: a wall, *impenetrable---insurmountable;* darkness is upon me!

Fragile man whose spirit longs to be free---and is taught from within---look up, look *in and rest.* Call upon the Father---it is *just another test---another plateau* along the way.

Learn to trust and not *beat your breast---*You walk not alone! You are on your way home, child of Mine; view the path from above. See it from my Son's perspective and *love each bump along the way!*

Concentrate on loving---concentrate on Him. Watch the road *flatten out* before your eyes. You could not stand, nor could you act upon the complete lane of the surface road ahead of you.

Your training now requires bumps---and lumps in the road---forcing you to read and pray until your programmed mind longs to praise Me and seek My face!

As you continue to review, the distance lengthens between each furrow---enabling you to stand tall for Me viewing the *souls along the way.* Gather them up for Me and walk on ---O son, O daughter.

Walk on---walk on---victory belongs to Me.

ABBA   12-11-82

DANGER OF SHRINKING BACK

Hebrews 10:26
    If we keep deliberately keep on sinning after we
    have received the knowledge of the truth, no
    sacrifice for sins is left...

My children---I bring to your attention a very serious matter this day, to check your core beliefs.

Can you, like Joshua of old, say to others with confidence: "Choose for yourselves this day whom you will serve...But as for me and my household, we will serve the Lord." (Joshua 24:15) If you are unwilling to obey the Lord, then decide today whom you will obey!

This is the same question I ask of you today. Have you decided to serve Me without question---go where I tell you to go and put Me first, letting Me guide you in all of your decision making?

Are you, like King David, and other followers of My Son who said upon rising each morning, "Lord---tell me clearly what to do today, in service to You, and dear Lord please tell me where to turn ---that I might serve Your greater needs this day?"

Ask me anything in line with Your Word this day. Help me to believe the unseen days ahead, totally trusting You to guide me along Your path!

Have you, My child, started to waiver, and become distant to My teaching? Have you forsaken the study of My Word each day---with loss of prayer for your several needs---and stopped praising Me?

For I have said, "I inhabit the praises of My children." Do you come to worship with the body of Christ each Lord's day? Do you seek others and pray together to intercede for a brother or sister? Or do you just go about your life, each day---without *once* having a quiet time with Me to reflect on your life?

When you don't include Me in your life's decisions, you will fall prey to Satan's attacks.

Have you known forgiveness in the past, and being fortified in the Word---lost track of everything---especially *My guidance*?

O! Dear children---come back to your first beginnings, and return to the *path of forgiveness*; for when you turn again to Me in *true obedience* and *repentance*, I will put your *past sins* behind Me and remember them *no more!*

Come back to the *water of life*, and I will guide you for the rest of your days, even to rest in My heavenly home--- after your time on earth is over!

DEEP SEATED ANGER

Psalm 37:8-9

Refrain from anger and turn from wrath; do not fret—it leads only to evil. For evil men will be cut off, but those who hope in the LORD will inherit the land.

Deep seated anger, the harbinger of death! I make a pronouncement, " All who harbor such anger are full of rage."

Where does this anger come from? Stop and consider, loved one, it does not come from Me. It comes from *inflicted pain*, real or imagined. Can you pin point the source?

There is a fracture in the road ---loved on---between you and Me. Perfect love casts out fear (1 Jn. 4:18). You my children harbor fear and resentment, like building blocks, stone upon stone, layer upon layer, until the wall that you have built day by day, year by year---has now clouded your vision---so that you see neither Me nor My Glory, paid for and complete, through the eye of your twisted and torn spirit!

Yes, it is true that you suffered in your early youth ---by the hands of another.

You then became the object of their rage, and so you too now repeat *in kind*. "The sins of the fathers are visited upon the sons." (Exodus 34:7) Is it possible to break the chain? Only by seeking the object of your God-given affection implanted in your inner man by Me!

For dear suffering one---know that I AM the object of your affection. Only I can restore tenderness to your wounded heart. Now---I say to you in strongest terms--- *repent,*

You who have given your allegiance to My Son, you who long for peace, and tenderness from a hurting spouse and others, repent of your evil thoughts toward them.

Others, like you, who have suffered *in kind*---know to do right. I give to each one of My creations, freedom of *will*. Now give it over to Me, and I will supply all your needs.

If, in your deep-seated anger, by your actions----not by your spouting of religious words to impress others--- you hold back, reserving the right to *hit out* at love offered to you; then angry one---your spiritual death will be slow and painful!

Wake up. Quit playing the jester on one hand, and acting like a demon on the other! "A double minded man is unstable in all his ways!" (Jam. 1:8)

So I say to you, "Draw near to Me and I will draw near to you." (Jam. 4: 8) Cleanse your heart and hands. Christ paid for the sins of mankind---once for all.

Quiet self; take the time to get alone with Me. You will find *peace* and *rest,* and a life filled with *new beginnings* for you and yours, fit for the Master's use. Bring others into a state of love, forgiveness, and service. Thereby is My love fulfilled!

ABBA

DESPITEFULLY USED

1 Cor. 6:9-10

Do you not know that the wicked will not inherit the kingdom of God? Do not be deceived: Neither the sexually immoral nor idolaters nor adulterers nor male prostitutes nor homosexual offenders nor

thieves nor the greedy nor drunkards nor slanderers
nor swindlers will inherit the kingdom of God.

Are you living with the consequences of wicked men?
Have you suffered at the hands of those who do evil? Do
you grieve for those around you who are suffering because
of the evil you see?

Pray for those who despitefully use you. Pray for their
spirit; pray for their health (mental and physical). Pray for
an awakening from their satanic promptings.

Pray for your own hearts as I invade your inner place of
rest and tranquility, as I focus My light, healing and power;
there I will do a cleaning of your house (*your inner man*) in
which your soul dwells.

I am not asleep ---as outward circumstances appear *to
you*, nor dull of hearing ---but weave a covering of
protection over you, and over your loved ones, children of
My Love!

ABBA   9-12-89

DIRECTIONS FOR RUNNING THE RACE

Hebrews 12:1
Therefore, since we are surrounded by such a
great cloud of witnesses, let us throw off everything
that hinders and the sin that so easily entangles, and
let us run with perseverance the race marked out for
us.

The race you have begun is already won. Why O why . . .
will you not *cross over the finish line.* Rise up---Come sit
before Me, for you are *in need of great teaching*---when at
its story's end, will bring a . . . *great releasing!*

For He paid it all, as they stretched Him tall. He paid it all for you. Stretch your faith---and believe. You are worthy in Me!

I cleansed you and made you white as snow. Now get on your knees and pray—*It was all settled long ago.*

ABBA

DISOBEDIENT CHILD

1 Tim. 1:9
   We also know that law is made not for good men but for lawbreakers and rebels, the ungodly and sinful, the unholy and irreligious; for those who kill their fathers or mothers, for murders...

Rave on O raging one--- rave on! Your flesh is determined to dominate your spirit, at times, to the point of *no return!* Why do you choose to die? Repent and return to your God. Make a covenant of peace with your maker.

   Rave on O raging one---rave on..."All have sinned"--- all have turned away. (Rom. 3:23) All have used their own mighty arm. The arm withers---the heart grows faint and weary.

   Conniving and lawlessness appears as *fear.* It is allowed to be nourished under the flesh of man in *total rebellion* oblivious to My call on their lives.

   I know what man is made of, and also what man is capable of. He can rise to the heights of heaven or sink to the deepest of pits! It is time to arise, My child, and time to receive *knowing forgiveness.*

   Are you aware---have you really sought My face? Have you actually sought My Son? I demand that you cease from your lawlessness and senseless fears.

   Reach out with the faith that is within you, and come *home to the nest of love---joy---peace* and an apportionment

48

of eternal riches. They await the *repentant heart.* Your true joy and sanctuary lies in the light of the Son.

I say, "Repent!" Receive My Son while you still have time. *Stop your lawlessness.* Seek My face---seek My glory---Seek My joy. Frame your existence within the confines of My Word; then the glory of the Lord your *God will be upon you*---even in prophetic ways!

My love knows no bounds of forgiveness to an *obedient---repentant heart.*

ABBA

DIVINE GRACE

John 14:6
Jesus answered, "I am the way, the truth, and the life. No one comes to the Father except through me."

Your days are numbered with *Divine Grace*---as are the days of all mankind, and I will receive you to Myself when the *work* that *I have called you to do is finished.* Much work remains to be done. You will have a long and fruitful life in Me only as long as you remain in the *work*---guided by My hand!

Do not cast doubt upon *these* words—be faithful— believe--search the Word. Many have come this far and have *fallen back*; it will not be so with you!

Redeem the time for the days are short and the nights are long spent.

Be not high minded; remember that you were 'bought back' to the Father by the blood of the Lamb; now trust in the triune God: Father, Son, and Holy Spirit who was and is and ever shall be.

ABBA

DO NOT FEAR WHAT MAN CAN DO

Psalm 118:6
> The LORD is with me; I will not be afraid.
> What can man do to me?

I have reserved for Myself a remnant who continues to throw their lives into the fray (struggle) . . . for Me.

I do, at times, command the *waves* and *storms of life* to be still. I exercise My power as I will but----O! How I long to sup with you and chat awhile, to see in your eyes the longing for My presence.

O! Man---O! Woman, wrap your mantle about your frame and see Me there, up ahead, along the path of life.

For I go before you *as of old.* I go before you and prepare the precious *Kingdom* jewels of life (righteousness, peace, and joy in the Holy Spirit!)

Think it not strange I cause you to walk this same path. For out of suffering---your faith in Me is born. For out of *suffering* your life is torn from your hands to *depend on* Me!

ABBA

DO YOU HAVE A ZEAL FOR GOD

Romans 10:2
> For I can testify about them that they are zealous
> for God, but their zeal is not based on Knowledge.

Do you have a zeal for God? Are you one who is waiting for correspondence from one you love with all your heart, body and soul--- who is in the world, but not within your sight?

Do you love your father God and soak in His Word---praying for more and more understanding as you read His love letters to you?

Or do you only have a nodding acquaintance with Him, paying lip service to the Lord of the universe?

Most of My church-going children don't stop and speak to Me as they go about their busy daily lives.

Are your days too crowded with work and painfully trying to balance your checkbook, and taking care of your own children?

Yes, and concerned with the nonbelievers and some Christian's *in name only*? Even some are experimenting with a world full of drugs today.

O! Loved ones---if all of this message strikes close to your heart, call on Me, and I will answer you, opening your hearts, minds and souls to the hidden things, and fenced in things--- in the scriptures, waiting for you to comprehend and understand your very existence. (Jer. 33:3)

I will show you things that you do not know. O! Come to the water of life and I will satisfy your thirst; for the water that I will give you---will become in you, a fountain of water *springing up into* everlasting *life* (Jn. 4:14).

So come My beloveds---come to Me--I will satisfy all of your needs!

ABBA   8-3-09

DO YOU HEAR THE CALL

Romans 9:25

As he says in Hosea: " I will call them 'my people,' who are not my people; and I will call her 'my loved one' who is not my loved one."

51

Changing scenes and passing dreams---Do you hear the call? Do you hear the wind as it carries My song? Do you hear the challenging call, "Launch out---launch out---reach for the song of the ages"?

All who can hear the sound of the trumpet, energize your faith, and move with its call.

Put man in the shadows and hear My clear sound. Liken it to the bells of old---as they chime for you. Step forth--- step out, I have *parted your red sea.* Walk on---listen closely to My voice.

I have much to say through you. I have much to pray through you. Your ministry: To nurture, to build, to stand in the gap---with armor in place. Step out in faith and grasp the hand of Him (Jesus) who leads you to My throne.

I have called a remnant to Faith in the unseen. Only My light and presence will lead you this day---and even forevermore!

Continue in your praises to Me, continue in your prayers, continue in the discernment of the written word.

A pure warning I give this day---look not back to that city of *changing scenes* and *passing dreams.*

There are three keys on a ring---dangling over a red heart: Hope---Faith---and Charity. This is a door of new beginnings. Insert each key into its proper slot---Turn them all together.

Open the door of new beginnings as you walk into the unseen. The light---His light will illumine your way. See His sign---"This is the way---walk you in it!"

I have given you new wine this day---be sure you put it in new wine skins!

ABBA   8-14-88

DO YOU WANT TO BE MADE WELL

John 5:6
When Jesus saw him lying there and learned that he had been in this condition for a long time, he asked him, "Do you want to get well?"

You walk---you strive---walking through life as one who is as good as dead! You are like the man with an infirmity! I said to him, "Do you want to be made well?" Then have your faith in Me.

Dear reader---you need to have faith and trust in Me; when you ask for prayer---*be specific.* When you are approached by a person needing prayer, whether for physical concerns or in other areas, establish immediately that you are going to pray for their specific need with faith and trust that I will answer their request.

Tell them that they too must receive your prayer also in faith and trust. (Mk. 9:23-24) In plain English: This is the formula that I will answer in the affirmative

Now! Continue to believe for your own healing---in your own times of need. Step out in obedience and pass this message on to others *who walk without hope!*

Use your wellness as a guiding light to all who would be made well. Remember---"One with an experience is never at the mercy of another with an *argument!"*

Keep that simple undying trust in Me, knowing that I love to give good gifts to My children who live in *obedience* and a lifestyle of *repentance.*

These *two words* are the keys that *unlock* My heart. So *well one*---this is your *call* to service! Show them that I still answer prayer; as when I asked the man with an infirmity---this question: "Do you want to be healed?"

ABBA   8-3-09

EARTHBOUND NO MORE

1 Cor. 15:22
For as in Adam all die, so in Christ all will be
made alive.

Come---take My hand as we stroll the lanes of My universe
viewing the expansive creation; note the children playing
amongst the clouds. Listen to their voices---O! See how
they play!

Earth-bound *no more*---these are the children who,
while on earth for just a very short time, were in such *need
of repair.* I called them home---in a moment of time, drew
them to My bosom and declared, "Rest, rest dearest ones---
rest now upon My breast."

Now free to roam, and grow in wisdom and strength. I
know, beloved, how you miss their presence after giving
them a home inside your womb, and the disappointment
you feel over your loss!

All is not lost; you will see them again and be drawn to
their side---exploring the wonders of heaven together.

You did nothing wrong---so don't punish yourself. You
will have an eternity together to get to know them---in the
purest sense, freed from worldly entanglements.

Trust Me, loved one---trust that I care about this world
you live in, with all of life's uncertainties. It will seem but
a blink of an eye as you view My kingdom of love!

Be at rest beloved ---I, even I, *redeem the time!*

ABBA   6-30-09

EMPOWERED BY THE SPIRIT

Titus 3:5

...he saved us not because of righteous things we had done, but because of his mercy. He saved us through the washing of rebirth and renewal by the Holy Spirit...

Dear child of Mine, I know you have a great love for Me---yet I have this much against you. Though you are still in the flesh---growing day by day in knowledge and the truth, spending the time searching the scriptures for the hidden and fenced in things in My Word, you still, at times feel like a failure-- unable to live the Christian life.

Beloved child, when this fear comes over you---realize where this fear is coming from. Satan's prime priority is to bring fear into your lives, and if nurtured it will bring you into a state of *guilt.*

He will also accuse you of not measuring up to My standards of living the Christian life---and on and on, until you realize and sense the sound of his hiss. Know that the accusations are from him ---*the father of lies!*

Your inner man lets you know in your heart of hearts that Jesus died and rose again, paying the price on the cross for your release. You know that I have forgiven you as you, in obedience and repentance, are brought back into fellowship with Me!

Stay on the alert at all times and know that I never sleep; neither does the Holy Spirit and your personal angel, who will guide you through the hard and lonely times---until the day I bring you home out of the dark tunnels of life on earth into everlasting life and light when you will see Me face to face, and I will see you face to face!

ABBA   8-7-09

ENDURE GOD'S CHASTENING

Hebrews 12:5-6

And have you forgotten that word of encouragement that addresses you as sons: "My son, do not make light of the Lord's discipline and do not lose heart when he rebukes you, because the Lord disciplines those he loves, and he punishes everyone he accepts as a son."

Have you been disciplined lately? Is there a root of bitterness about you? Does it upset you when the goals you set for your life have not materialized?

Did that cause you to blame your circumstances on others, or even worse ---on Me---your Lord and Savior!

In quiet revenge---have you stopped coming to church regularly, being in church fellowship---a or a small home group fellowshipping with your brothers or sisters in Me?

If your answer is yes to all or part of the above, I tell you beloveds---*chastening is in order!*

I have said in My love letters (Bible) to My children, "If you endure chastening, I will deal with you as with sons and daughters."

For what son or daughter is there whom a father does not chasten? (Heb. 12:7) I want you to be all that you can be--- in Me--- fit for service in the fight for common man, who doesn't know the reality of kingdom living in this battered and fallen world. Endure My chastening and come back to Me. I will guide your life and use you in service to Me, aiding in the recovery of mankind---free of Satan's attacks. O! The things I have in store for you, things for good and not for evil, to give you a future and a hope!

Come back to your heritage O! Redeemed one, and as you do I will bring you to My table of grace when you depart from this world of pain and suffering; and once again I will gird Myself and wash your feet!

Come and dine---*even now*---at My communion table---O! Forgiven one!

ABBA   7-25-09

EXTENDED TIME

Psalm 37:25

I was young and now I am old, yet I have never seen the righteous forsaken or their children begging bread. They are always generous and lend freely; their children will be blessed.

I have brought you into the extended time of your lives, time when it has been My good pleasure for you to stand as a light ---an oasis---for a people in this younger generation who are hungering for the taste of the reality of Me that they have never known before.

Watch and see, in the years of your lives still to come, the mantle of understanding, the needs, the dilemma, and the lost-ness of some who have fallen from grace.

But through your prayers of deliverance, they are enabled to step out in faith, and be restored to My Body---the living church, actively cooperating with the Church body, becoming *lights* on a *hill, a* place where *Living* Water is poured-out in truth and righteousness, spreading to and through the borders of this state ---to the far reaches of lands now hampered by the hoards of hell itself!

So---dear ones, I use you to be pillars of strength and wisdom in this wicked and perverse world--- for Me!

Some---even now---are following along in your foot steps---as they see and have noted your passion for My blessed Son and Holy Spirit, who continues to use you ---as He wills!

Continue to serve Me and man, for their good, and above all---"For My Glory!"

ABBA   12-18-92

FAST AND PRAY BEFORE ANY MISSION

Isaiah 58:6

Is not this the kind of fasting I have chosen: to loose the chains of injustice, to untie the cords of the yoke, to set the oppressed free and break every yoke?

Any mission I cause you to accept must be primed and ready for direction---after prayer and fasting.

Tell her, tell him, that (through repentance and obedience to My Word) their prayers are heard and acted upon with *fire!*

Now---place, by faith, the torch of the Spirit's flaming fire in the direction of My leading. Help the blind to see.

Never let it once be named among you that you are worthless and defeated! Do not listen to the voice of the accuser.

I place My protective hand over you. Go forth into the battle for the minds of man, armor in place; armed with fire from Me. O! Child of My tree---stand, and watch Me fight on your behalf for the lives you came to set free--- in Me.

ABBA   3-16-80

FOR A VERY SPECIAL LADY

Prov. 31: 10-12

A wife of noble character who can find? She is worth far more than rubies. Her husband has full confidence in her and lacks nothing of value. She brings him good, not harm all the days of her life.

Dearest lady full of grace---prayers on your behalf have risen to My father's heart.

I know your fears, your concerns, your joys, and aspirations for your husband and children; now My light is turned upon you.

Little flower of My heart---I know the potential that lies within you---- the gift of harmony---sometimes at the cost of your own comfort. You have gone that extra mile to preserve harmony within your family and those close and dear to you, causing you to tilt toward despair.

Look to My Word and remember you are not without hope; pause and think about this word, "You will keep in perfect peace him whose mind is steadfast, because he trusts in you." (Is. 26:3)

You have the gift of loyalty; so few in and out of My grasp are loyal! Cultivate this gift; in so doing you bring honor to My name!

You have a latent gift of creativity; exercise and expand this gift even to enfold the needs of the body of Christ and His church wherein you worship!

From your household---concentrate on the support and encouragement of your husband; also he through his love for you and in obedience to My word must concentrate on supporting and encouraging you two together.

Then this godly blend will cause others to seek your council.

Until I come---join the *faithful few* who dare to risk all for the furtherance of the *good news*: That I came to seek and save all the who-so-ever-wills.

Exercise the potential deep within you and know that I will never leave you. Know this---believe this, I look for you to blossom forth in faith and trust in your sure resurrection, joining those that have gone on before you in *newness of life*. I love and preserve you O! Faithful one!

ABBA   6-4-97

FORTIFIED STRONGHOLDS

2 Cor. 10:4
The weapons we fight with are not the weapons of the world. On the contrary, they have divine power to demolish strongholds.

Do not be concerned over what seems to be a fortified strong- hold. The battle rages on---but I AM in control.

Your angels never tire. Their swords of fire have been bloodied from battling the hoards of demons that have been thrown against you.

But---dear child of My heart---We prevail together. Carry on the mission I have given you of bringing people out of confusion and despair. Follow the pursuits of My heart in bringing still others, in like circumstance, to My Son.

Keep on, dearest one, with your *straightforward approach*---which is penetrating their *stiff-necked* hearts! What a force for the kingdom they will become as a result of your longsuffering approach in sharing My word with them.

Guide them along to the healing of all their memories past and present. Do you see now, sweet child, why I have given you these latest assignments bringing the hoards of hell your way?

But I AM your shield and buckler. I bring you through the battle---alive and well!

So carry on---O! Flower of My heart. Remember to put on your armor daily. The battle rages on, and you are in the midst of it---standing *behind Me*---as I walk you through the minefields!

ABBA   6-8-82

FORTIFY YOURSELVES

Psalms 27:14
Wait on the Lord; Be of good courage, And he shall strengthen your heart; Wait, I say, on the Lord!

Fortify yourselves with the Word for within that *fortified environment,* surrounded by My *living word* and *member saints* in the *church triumphant,* you will *know* your placement and so draw strength and guidance given by My hand, and thereby receive *wisdom* to carry out your appointed tasks from My strong right hand.

As troubled hearts seek sanctuary in your presence and guidance from My *living word*, truth and comfort will flow from your lips, quieting troubled, confused, and desperate hearts.

Hearts are failing the *young* as well as the *old* as they stumble into your sanctuary (home) looking for answers to their fears and frustrations.

Be wise as serpents and harmless as doves, always remembering their *fragile frame of mind.*

Never, never give *quick answers* to their dilemmas; *always seek* My *divine guidance.* As you do this, then the *anointed* answer *will come!*

ABBA

GOD HOLDS YOUR BREATH IN HIS HANDS

Daniel 5:23b
. . you did not honor the God who holds in his hands your life and all your ways.

Beloveds---be not *high minded*; for you were made in My likeness and bought with a price, and you are not your own. (1 Cor. 6:20) You were fearfully and wonderfully made. (Ps. 139:14)

Made for the express purpose of serving Me, your Lord and king! You live and breathe---in service to Me. You are a living rock---chosen by Me for kingdom service, along with your earthly needs. (1 Pet. 2:4)

Give Me your *wills*, to My care and keeping. I have also given you a wide range of activity in your lives; created you to be a spiritual and fleshly being, both working in perfect harmony!

Then came Satan and his demons to disrupt and try to claim you for himself! You were created a free moral agent with the freedom of choice.

You may choose life in Me, or death and separation from My kingdom. So carry on in your flesh life--- with the knowledge that I AM light, and not darkness.

Work and live in the *forever now* as *resident aliens*, serving Me and mankind in your daily pursuits; for your *daily pursuits* are a natural part of your lives here on earth; but do not let them take over your lives--- with very little time left in service to Me!

Take the time, while in service to Me, to seek and enjoy the honest earthly pleasures coupled with faith and trust in Me.

Enjoy these pleasures in moderation. Ask--- as did King David of old, upon rising from sleep each day, "Lord tell me clearly what to do today, and which way to turn."

My child ---I will always guide you safely through Satan's minefields.

Always live your lives in a state of obedience to My written words, and live a lifestyle of repentance when you miss the mark and sin.

Choose your activities carefully, and remember—loved one--- *I, even I, hold your breath in My hands!*

ABBA 8-1-09

GOD'S AIM FOR THE CHURCH

Eph 4:12-13

Why is it that He gives us these special abilities to do certain things best? It is that God's people will be equipped to do better work for Him, building up the church, the body of Christ, to a position of strength and maturity; until finally we all believe alike about our salvation, and about our Savior, God's Son, and all become full grown in the Lord---yes, to the point of being filled full with Christ. *Selah* [LIV]

What does it profit a man to gain the world, and lose his own soul? Brothers and sisters, we are called to live by a higher standard than *non-believers*, counting the cost, then launching out on the *waters of life* into the most rewarding occupation: a fully dedicated life.

Living for the Trinity to serve all of mankind! What an awesome assignment for you, My child!

You are called to live, in service to your Father God as *resident aliens*---doing the work, as did Jesus, who laid down His life in order to bring you back to His Father, and yours!

To serve the who-so-ever-wills, the Father will cause these true seekers to cross your paths. Always be ready to give an answer for the *hope that is within you. You* will know in your heart of hearts that you are under His direction, along with His assigned angels, who see to your every need, which includes *suffering for Him.*---This is a *heavenly tool* which will define the difference between the soulless man and the spiritual man within the complexities between the two (soul and spirit).

I guide your very existence as you toil for Me on this earth, wooing and winning as many as you can for the cause of the Kingdom, living with Me in the forever now--- even throughout all eternity!

ABBA   7-3-09

GOD'S REASON FOR OUR SUFFERING

2 Tim. 2:8

...This is my gospel, for which I am suffering even to the point of being chained like a criminal.... I endure everything for the sake of the elect, that they too may obtain the salvation that is in Christ Jesus, with eternal glory.

If we endure, we will also reign with him. If we disown him, he will also disown us....

God---our Father allows us to go through suffering to burn off the *worldly dross* that accumulates and so easily binds and blinds us!

My children ---let Me give you an illustration of the dross that covers and stifles My children.

You may have in your garden a beautiful rose bush called the
Knock-Out rose bush. It requires very little maintenance as it grows and produces various colored roses.

But---to keep growing new flowers it requires constant pruning. As you see the flowers begin to fade and die, you must take your clippers and cut off the dead and dying ones.

Then the plant will grow while suffering the shock of the pruning process. For a short spell, most of the plant is without flowers.

This sturdy plant recovers from the shock and begins again to grow and flourish once again with beautiful new roses for all to see and enjoy!

Life is like that, dear ones, in order to continue to grow and be at your game best, I *allow suffering* to keep you looking unto Me, as did Jesus in the days that He suffered for the *sins of common man.*

I allowed Him to go through the hurts and stings, and loneliness, in the garden while His closest friends slept!

Man treated My Son in despicable ways---and finally nailed Him to the Cross.

You don't have to go through such torture, love one, but I remind you, that in your own flesh---I never allow your suffering to go beyond what each of you can bear!

I AM the one who 'snips off' the dross from your life that is built up day by day: The disappointments, the

65

physical suffering of your body and mind, the sins of your past, your heavy burdens, and wasted time.

Note that through the power of prayer and praise, I can lead you into healthy living, while in service to Me.---So, dear reader, if you are in that state of suffering, be it physical or mental, come before Me in all humility. Remember, all My promises are true, *but conditional* ---on obedience to My Word, and a lifestyle of *repentance.*

Do these things, and I will *renew you*, clipping off the old dead flowers and freeing you to start over in service to Me. Let your fresh new roses shine, and may the people closest to you and *those from afar*--- take heart.

And the aroma from heaven will fill the air about you as you walk in service to Me, helping the who-so-ever-wills to come to an understanding---why I have allowed you to *suffer in My Name.*

And when your allotted time on this planet is over, come sit with Me---The father of light---meet and greet all of your loved ones that have gone ahead of you into eternity---sharing together--- forever---all of eternity!

ABBA   7-14-09

GREATER WORKS SHALL YOU DO

John 14:12-13

I tell you the truth, anyone who has faith in me will do what I have been doing. He will do even greater things that these, because I am going to the Father. And I will do whatever you ask in my name, so that the Son may bring glory to the Father.

I have commissioned you to do these greater works; daily take up your cross and do the work that I have called you to do!

I sit now firmly at the right hand of My father---receiving your prayer requests with the father. Live in an atmosphere of praise along with your prayers.

I AM always just a heartbeat away. Start out each day in total submission to My *will*, and I will chart the path ahead of you, and will tell you where to stop and rest!

Do not launch out on your own; for I will open doors that are shut--- doors of opportunity that you do not know!

Souls of man are failing them; your present government has become a cesspool of self-serving men and women drunk with power to capture your *will* and bring it into submission. Never fear, My children ---I have not abdicated My throne to Satan's children, who are destined for the flames of torment--- in hell!

I have called the *well informed* that are close to My breast and heart---to go into all the world, searching for captured hearts, and setting them free.

No time for self-exaltation---running here and there looking for peace and contentment. My child---WE are at war---and the air is filled with Satan's hoards.

O! Wicked and perverse children---as in the days of Sodom and Gomorrah---their bodies filled with lust, that comes out of the pits of hell to tempt man to sin against Me.

Send out the young in years, filled with vitality, with clean hearts and minds that are controlled by My Spirit partnering with theirs to finish the work of bringing the who-so-ever-wills to Me.

With an eye toward their heavenly kingdom (of righteousness, peace, and joy in the Holy Spirit), and with prayer and praises on their lips, they please Me and trust

My ways for their lives in the administration of My selective duties for them!

So walk, and work, in obedience to the light of the Word!

ABBA   8-10-09

GUARDIAN ANGELS

Psalm 91:11
… For He will command his angels concerning you to guard you in all your ways.

Have you ever tested the existence of My angels sent to guard you? I want you to be aware of how securely you are protected by their actions on your behalf…Of how inside the realm of the spiritual world the battle rages on! They, with your guided prayers, hold off the enemy of your souls.

As blessed children of the King, you have the right, authority--and duty to call upon your angels to guard and protect you.

Know this---you are *never alone.* When in obedience to Me you call out in believing prayer, legions of angelic beings are at your beck and call!

How diligently they pursue the dark forces. O! How dark the outer system is without My protective light. Even those in rebellion against Me are kept safe from the fallen one. His *hate is almost in proportion to My love.*

For My love spans all of eternity!

Such intensity---only because I hold total power is he kept at bay! Now that you are becoming more aware of the nearness of Me, and My angels' support, reach out and strengthen their hands and efforts. Read, praise, and pray. That is the key to My ever listening ear!

So watch and continue to pray---be aware of the struggle that continues on your behalf. Salvation is *not* the issue. Fruitful service is!

ABBA 2-12-84

Isaiah 63:9
In all their distress he too was distressed, and the angel of his presence saved them. In his love and mercy he redeemed them; he lifted them up and carried them all the days of old.

Daniel 3:28
Then Nebuchadnezzar said, "Praise be to the God of Shadrach, Meshach, and Abednego, who has sent His angel, and rescued His servants! They trusted in him and defied the king's command and were willing to give up their lives rather than serve or worship any god except their own God."

HALLOWED HANDS—HALLOWED HEART

Rev 12:11
They overcame him by the blood of the Lamb and by the word of their testimony; they did not love their lives so much as to shrink from death.

Hallowed hands---Hallowed heart, you received My Words from the start. Never doubt in times of testing---that I never fail to test your metal.

See the world in utter sin, corrupt and callous from within. Shapeless voids of blackest night bring patches of despair.

You are called upon now without seeing up ahead. I know the feeling you have this day---daring, at last for Me to have My way---*so few step onto this path!*

Watch the honorable man---his way is peace. No need for him to require a fleece, for he trusts the *great I AM!*

I AM He, EL Shaddai, I AM He---It is Me---it is I who works for you this day, grafting to My Tree that righteous man now covered by My blood. I AM He who gives life---I AM He who takes it away!

I require you to pray and praise---to stand in the gap for common man---who cannot stand on his own! The din of the world is heavy to one's ears.

Who cares to listen when I call? It is you, dear beloved one, who hears My whispered voice as I speak to your heart and say, "Come---take your rest, and stand apart from the pull of the world. Watch him--- watch her that is obedient to the call."

True to themselves are they, ready to speak a word in or out of season---ready to risk all for the sake of My Son. I make others to follow their path. I make others---now free of Satan's grasp to forsake all ---and turn My way.

It is I who redeem the time---It is I, yes I, who has set you apart for a special work for Me; for you see, O hallowed hands and heart, I soon do a new thing in you---We are burning off the dross... Be clean be clean—Come now--- and rest in Me!

ABBA   3-15-84

HANDS THAT OPPOSE YOU

Luke 1:74-75

...to rescue us from the hand of our enemies, and to enable us to serve him without fear in holiness and righteousness before him all our days.

My hand is strong against those who would oppose you. I Am, and have made a clear path in the direction of your continuing ministry.

I---not man, guide your destination. I---not those who would oppose My plan for you, have destined your continuing ministry toward the expansion of My kingdom.

Continue sowing the seed of My word. Bless those in seclusion---bless those in confusion; make good use of the Word. Sooth their pain with the *Balm of Gilead* (ointment used to sooth wounds). *(Jer. 51:8)

Make straight the people's path---Continue to observe the unfolding of My prophetic plan; for in the unfolding--- you draw nearer to My hand----*fear not!*

ABBA   1-20-91

HARVEST TIME

John 4:35
Do you not say, "Four months more and then the harvest"? I tell you, open your eyes and look at the fields! They are ripe for harvest.

All those who hear My *Spirits heart* cry out, "Rescue them!" Are you ready? Stand strong, loved ones! See the throngs about you grasping, tearing at one another to catch a thread of your garments, for they sense an inner glow about your countenance.

They fall prey to every enticing thing in the world. *They grasp* but cannot get. *They get* but cannot keep. They weep

71

and cannot sleep; then they---*dream*. For them the *nightmare begins;* stress and despair overtakes them.

Check your armor in the light of My Word; wear it well. Increase the swell of them entering into My habitation. What abounding joy as we 'Toll the Bell' each time 'one'---*even one* is rescued!

From My hands to yours I pass the peace. From your hands to theirs: entwine, encourage, save and admonish; start a flourish, yes, even a landslide! For I dwell within you . . . to direct your hands, feet, and mouth.

ABBA

Psalm 126:6

He who goes out weeping, carrying seed to sow, will return with songs of joy, carrying sheaves with him.

Matthew 9:37

Then he said to his disciples, "The harvest is plentiful but the workers are few. Ask the Lord of the harvest, therefore, to send out workers into his harvest field."

Galatians 6: 9

Let us not become weary in doing good, for at the proper time we will reap a harvest if we do not give up.

HAVE YOU CAUGHT THE VISION

Proverbs 29:18

Where there is no revelation, the people cast off restraint; but blessed is he who keeps the law.

You, who have caught the vision, go into your prayer closet---away from the hustle and bustle of the day. Quiet yourself. Wait on the Spirit. He will open your heart to receive the urgent needs of the day in persons, places, and things. Keep a pad and pencil beside you, for the list may be long---*at times.*

Never be in a hurry to *rush through a prayer request* to Me. Let us sit together in the *Spirit* and converse. Seek My mind in all things. Know that you receive wise council from My Father's heart.

Let those who are very dear and close to you hear your praises of how I have answered your prayers for them for their recent *set backs* --- as they were passed on to Me, O faithful one!

Let them feel the intensity of your prayers as they were being made free *from the entanglements of this world.* For Christ has announced, by His death on the cross, that He has set them free---*fulfilling the law,* and now all eternity is theirs to explore--- the very day that I call them home.

ABBA

1 Thes. 5:17-18
Pray without ceasing. In everything give thanks; for this is the will of God in Christ concerning you.

HE BROUGHT US OUT

Deut. 6:23
And He brought us out from there to bring us in and give us the land that he promised on oath to our forefathers.

I have brought you out of your own self-made captivity in order that you would fulfill and use the gifts I have imparted to each and every one of you!

You are a unique person, made in My image with gifts within you to be used for My Glory and to bring other captives without hope or reason...to live their lives for Me,...making a marked difference to all those whom you touch for Me.

Be that light that I have caused you to be; you are still a developing flower of beauty but need more time growing in the soil of My love---soon to burst forth in beauty and grandeur!

Keep to the book---plumb its depths; live like one who is seeking the water of the living Lord!

Bring forth the well of refreshment; let its cool soothing water energize your body, soul and spirit---as you drink your fill.

For the water I give you will bring to your heart and soul new invigorating health and mental clarity. Let your energy show forth in *faith* and *trust* with full assurance that what you ask for will be birthed with newness of life.

For you, O obedient one, have captured the truth of My love for man. You have believed with all your heart that I will fulfill your needs!

And when you slip and go after the wrong goals rather than the ones I had for you to complete---you know to repent and walk in newness of life, determined to fulfill the tasks that I called you to do, nothing wavering as you cross the goal and complete your mission, in Jesus name, to save the lost of this world for Me!

Continue on, beloved, and walk one day into My waiting loving arms!

ABBA   9-10-09

HEALED BY GOD ALONE

Matthew 14:35b-36
People brought all their sick to him and begged
him to let the sick just touch the edge of his cloak,
and all who touched him were healed.

You have been healed for a purpose....
No healing is done without My hand in it! I know those
who are given over to Satan who makes it an unholy habit
to ruin the lives of My creation---if he can. It is to his
detriment---for the day is not far off, as I reckon time, when
he and his followers, that horde of demons who fell with
him,---will spend an eternity in the *lake of fire*! (Rev.
19:20)
He especially attacks and consumes the children giving
into drugs of their choice. Don't think that I delay; but it
has been given to you---the children of My Kingdom whom
I have called to pray: To *heal* in My Name, to love and
nurture them---and their parents.
Bring those who have been abandoned and left to their
devices. Bring them---by *word and deed* into the sanctuary
that they may find help in their *desperate time of need*!
When you call upon My Spirits healing power in
believing trust, I am free and just to work the work of
healing.
The enemy is strong...but has been overcome by the
blood of the lamb, (Rev. 7:14) dedicated to put God first in
lives, and will stand against the evil one until the end of
time, allowing the weaker sons and daughters to safely find
their way home!

ABBA

Isaiah 57:18-19

"I have seen his ways, but I will heal him; I will guide him and restore comfort to him, creating praise on the lips of the mourners in Israel. Peace, peace to those far and near," says the Lord. "And I will heal them."

HEALING THE MIND AND THE BODY

Matthew 4:23
    And Jesus went throughout Galilee, teaching in their synagogues, preaching the good news of the kingdom, and healing every disease and sickness among the people.

I am Sovereign---I AM true ---I do care, and long for you, as I long for all My children, to curl about My feet (spiritually).

To the Imperfect man in an imperfect world made to be whole by the Blood of the Lamb, I allow discomfort. It gets your attention---like no other way; it *always will*; but don't feel persecuted ---and please don't fret---you are not alone.

Let's talk about your present dilemma---*overeating*--- when in a state of despair. This is sin! Trust Me in your dilemma, and throw the weight of it all on Him---He carries it well. "Cast all your anxiety on him because he cares for you. Be self-controlled and alert." (1 Pet. 5:7-8a)

I touch you just now---feel the warmth of My caress. Be at rest---be at peace. Rest---relaxation is what you need. Go finish your 'work-a-day' tasks, and spend this evening at home---reading My Word---praying and praising My Name and be ready; for tomorrow is a new day filled with great possibilities. ---Just follow My leading!

ABBA   3-24-83

HEALTH ON THE MORROW

Deut. 7:15
The Lord will keep you free from every disease. He will not inflict on you the horrible diseases you knew in Egypt but he will inflict them on all who hate you.

Proverbs 3:6
In all your ways acknowledge Him, and He shall make your paths straight.

Bewildered and oft times out of sorts with Me and Man, loved one? Tests do come to try your metal and *grow you up*. If I seem harsh and unloving, it is needed, at times, and is a *sure way toward maturity* in your walk with Me. For loved one ---I need your feet to stand on *solid ground* in the defense for common man. Some of today's events have brought you to your knees.

The enemy is a coward and as such does most of his dastardly deeds when you least expect it! Do not mistake his *soon to be* position in hell as a retardant of his actions; for he will thwart, confuse, and steal all that man was made to be---*without quarter---* if he can.

I now bring you *peace* and *rest* for a healthy *tomorrow*: a day of untold solutions unfolding before your very eyes as you---with patience--- look to My Word before the start of each day. Put on your armor* before stepping out into your b*roken world*.

Give this day to Me, and I will show you the pathway. This honors and glorifies My Name.

ABBA

Eph. 6:11

Put on the full armor of God so that you can take your stand against the devil's schemes.

HIS HAND EXTENDED

Psalm 91:1-2

He who dwells in the shelter of the Most High will rest in the shadow of the Almighty. I will say of the Lord, "He is my refuge and my fortress, My God, in whom I trust."

Into your hands O Lord---into your hands I commit my being. As I stand firm upon the hills and valleys, I am aware of Your outstretched protective hands, reaching out over your creation.

I ponder this early morn on all that my eyes survey; for from His hands, worlds were formed across this seemingly endless universe---and beyond!

From Your hands, judgment was pronounced upon this earth. Your hands have made a way in the wilderness. Your hands have tilled the soil of the soul of man!

Yes! From Your hands, a co-existing branch (Jesus) was brought forth; and He swept the land and the people of Your pasture ---clean.

Let me know and be comforted by the knowledge that over this land of Your creation, are the everlasting arms that bear me up on this very rock (Jesus). I stand firm in the awareness that the hands that are supporting me---hold my life---which is not mine to command.

O! Father O! Guardian of my soul, know that I love you, and desire even more of Your Holy Spirit *by faith*, and *action,* in service to You and mankind.

Let me know that as I continue to walk along the paths and furrows that line Your *palms*, no matter where the lines cross---all lead to your heart of hearts.

Into Your hands O Lord----I commit my being!

ABBA   8-9-89

HOLY WORDS OF INSTRUCTION

John 7:38
Whoever believes in me, as the Scripture has said, streams of living water will flow from within him.

Let your day start with prayer and thanksgiving *fully armed with battle gear. You can make it a *holy habit* of devotions each morning---before walking out the door, be it for work or for play.

This brings honor to My Name and strength for the day!

As you grow in the 'living word' in *knowledge* of the scriptures---with wisdom, (Col. 4:5) make the most of your chance to tell others the good news.

Be wise and loving in all your contacts with them. I give you wise council in telling others---about the good news: Be wise as serpents and harmless as doves! (Mt. 10:16)

In all that you do and say, let Me remind you to guard well the *mouth of the river* that flows *in and through you*---purifying its water. Let no vain or dishonest thing proceed *out of your mouth!*

When you let your eyes stray from My guiding hand---and *fall, repent quickly*, clear the obstruction from the river, and once again let the *living water proceed out of your mouth.*

79

Guard yourselves from *worldly cares* or they will diminish your missions. (1 Cor. 7:23) Tell them of My precious promises. "You have been bought and paid for by Christ, so you belong to Him---be free from all these earthly prides and fears.

Go in peace and serve the Lord!

ABBA

*Eph. 6:10-13

Finally, be strong in the Lord and in his mighty power. Put on the full armor of God so that you can take your stand against the devil's schemes. For our struggle is not against flesh and blood, but against the rulers, against the authorities, against the powers of this dark world and against the spiritual forces of evil in the heavenly realms. Therefore put on the full armor of God so that when the day of evil comes, you may be able to stand your ground, and after you have done everything, to stand.

HOW DARE I SAY I SURRENDER NOT

Isaiah 53:6

We all, like sheep, have gone astray, each of us has turned to his own way; and the LORD has laid on him he iniquity of us all.

O God of my fathers, I *have strayed* from my God . . . but now in my despair and pain, I say, "Father, come quickly."

Wretched man that I am, you would have done it all for me alone---and so you have. *How dare I say—"I surrender not."* For as I lay prostrate before you I can say, "Surrender ends here and now. Victory and life lay before me—You and you alone are my healer my deliverer."

80

Cry victory, O man, . . . cry victory indeed. For in the victory celebration, healing follows. Come all who ponder: "Where does victory begin?" It begins in the basking in His beloved victorious arms, cradled and nestled in His care and keeping.

Fear not, little one of much worth, . . .*Fear not!* Return to Me, your Savior and Deliverer. I will never leave you nor forsake you. Live your life in obedience to Me!

I will bring you home to My kingdom when your allotted time on earth is completed.

In the mean time *lace*-up your shoes and go forth. Be on your way to capture for Me all the who-so-ever-wills that cross your path. Love on them, encourage them to read, praise, and pray; for I inhabit the praises of My children!

ABBA   10-14-81

I AM AN ALL CONSUMING FIRE

2 Thes. 1:6-8

God is just: He will pay back trouble to those who trouble you and give relief to you who are troubled...This will happen when the Lord Jesus is revealed from heaven in blazing fire with his powerful angels. He will punish those who do not know God and do not obey the gospel of our Lord Jesus.

A strong wind is blowing through the land. Beware of movers of deceit, you who gloss over the truth of My universal cry, "Consider the blameless, observe the upright; There is a future for the man of peace."

You who would make a mockery of justice, despicable ones given to Satanic lust for power to enslave the people of this land, your time for retribution is at hand!

I AM your retribution (nemesis) (one who inflicts punishment). You have gathered like killer bees to pounce on this beloved land---and people.

Instead, it is *you* I am collecting---like honey gone rancid. I am collecting you like the chaff you have *so willingly become.*

A fierce wind am I---fiercer then ten thousand hurricanes combined. My breath is scorching hot; for I AM an all-consuming fire. (Deut. 9:3)

The day of My wrath is at hand. See how the earth itself suffers and groans! Some of you will repent---*but not all.* The tragedy is that you have spoken lies for so long, you believe them *as the truth.*

Be concerned---those of you who are not precious 'followers of the way.'' History, once again, repeats itself as in many wicked nations before you. I have purged, and will continue to purge, the land and its people.

To you who sit in your churches---those who do not take-up My commission to read, praise, and pray; will also *be made* into a force of activity---called to pray, called to evangelize through your witness.

If you don't take heed---beware. For I AM weary of slothful, lazy children *who are asleep.* So lazy, so disobedient, that you are on the tip of My tongue to *spit you out!*

Wake-up, Wake-up I say. Wake-up to the heavenly call to be your brothers' and sisters' *keeper.*

ABBA

I BRING JOY AND VICTORY

Psalm 46:1
   God is our refuge and strength, an ever present help in trouble.

I AM bringing joy out of sadness and victory out of defeat this day, My child. You name the category of your concerns, and I, My children, am in the midst of them.

   I bring My strong right hand to touch areas of affliction---be they material or spiritual.

   I continue to bring shaking to the *so-called* intelligentsia: to those operating governments, large and small.

   This---My children, is just the beginning of trials and tribulations as My justice prevails *openly,* especially in governments; yes---even church governments also.

   The little people too are beginning to hear Me say, in effect, "The bell is chiming for you and you!"

   Touch their hearts at the level of their *understanding*; for the days are short---and the *long nights_*will soon be upon them.

   Read and study your Bible as never before---look around you. You already can see the signs of My coming again, this time, in Power---and Majesty. I will deal swiftly with those who are attempting to make slaves out of My people, casting them into the pit of perdition.

   I will not spare the rod! But to the faithful, long suffering children of Mine, I will take you to My bosom and return to My kingdom in victory.

   There you will forever enjoy the fruits of your earthly labor: seeking out the who-so-ever wills while in service to Me on planet earth! Rest now from your labors, beloveds!

ABBA   12-10-82

I LONG TO HAVE YOU BESIDE ME

Psalm 145:20
 The Lord preserves all them that love Him: but all the wicked will He destroy.

Blessed children---My heart is full to overflowing, as you---in love toward Me, in obedience, have coveted to follow Me.

 The burden of this war-torn world lies heavily upon My heart in the on-going turmoil of sick desolate nations who, in ignorance of My Word, war with one another.

 Such atrocities, born from the black heart of Satan and his demonic angels, continue---to this day to plague the world!

 Be bold in your witness to relatives and friends alike. Again I say, "Love the unlovely" For they---in their sin-filled conceit, dare to spill their disturbed hearts on those about them.

 In their sickness---they fail to come to the "Water of Life." They, in their pride, *will not come* that I might save and heal them!

 Trust Me as I---through you, show them the *pattern of life* that leads to My heavenly home! I say again, "Dare to be bold in your witness." Do you know, dear ones---how I long---even now, to draw you to My side in the heavenlies where we can talk face to face, and love on each other—forever. But I have need of you to stay here on this earth to gather all that you can into My Kingdom.

 Dark days again for all! Continue to be that light on My Hill---for you to be used as a launching pad—and path, to My Throne room.

 Rejoice loved one---rejoice, even as you dwell in the fire---for you will *"Never be burned by it."*

ABBA   4-18-02

I WILL SHOW MERCY ON WHOM I WILL

2 Chron. 30:9
> If you return to the Lord, then your brothers and your children will be shown compassion by their captors and will come back to this land, for the Lord your God is gracious and compassionate. He will not turn his face from you if you return to him.

I show mercy on whom I will, for I AM Christ the King. Glory, glory, He has set me free to go at His command---free to stand upon the sands of time viewing all humanity that passes by.

Night and day they do come---*but do they stay?* Do they dare to walk *your way?* Man was cursed before his birth when Adam and Eve fell in the Garden eons ago!

But Jesus paved the way. He took man's place upon that wooden cross---suspended between heaven and earth. Suspended indeed, until all had heard His cry of pain upon that rack!

A cry of pain as He looked into the black hours that man had devised. There was no other way to bring man back---back into the Father's fold.

For from of old---yes! from ancient of days---it was decided among We three, that no other way was left to Me--but to stretch My Son that you might live and be set free of Satan's grasp.

Free to come or go, free at last to exercise your will, for I made you thus! It was part of My plan that man should be free to reign with Me, a free-willed immortal soul. Now---truly Christ is ever interceding for you, O blessed one. Take your stand, you *blood-bought* man---O take your stand for Me.

For now you walk in the light of My love; for now you walk for Me. Be My hands, My feet, My life; continue to overcome for Me.

Always remember, and remind others too, that you *stand not alone.* As I go before you, continue to say, "Mercy, mercy, Christ the King---Glory, glory---He *has set me free."*

ABBA   7-1-83

IF ONE DOES NOT OBEY GOD

Hebrews 3:18
And to whom did God swear that they would
never enter his rest if not to those who disobeyed?

If one does not obey Me---there will be no rest for him or her. I Am sovereign---I AM eternal!

Your inner man---your body, soul, and spirit---will be in disarray, totally out of sync with My kingdom, and living without My daily, hour by hour, minute by minute---guidance!

You leave yourself with *no covering* and open to every wile (trick) of the enemy. I am a jealous God and will have no other gods before Me!

O! Finite man---I, and your warrior angels, cannot protect you if you continue on this path of disobedience and destruction---subject to every conceivable action that will surely come upon you.

I am shouting in your ear *to repent* and come into obedience; but you only hear My strong voice as a very *tiny whisper.*

Don't continue on in disobedience. I am patient and persistent, and am known as 'The Hound Of Heaven,' but

My patience will soon come to an end, and you will. If you do not---will not---come back to the father of lights, then total darkness will prevail!

I died on the cross and rose again on your behalf. I leave the door open to My throne of grace for your return, like the wayward son who asked for all of his inheritance, received it, and left his father's home, spending it in wildness and riotous living (Luke 15: 11-16). Having spent all, he found himself feeding with the hogs. When he came to his senses--- he returned to his father's home and asked for forgiveness.

O! Errant child come back to your *first love* and I will forgive you, clothing you with fine linen, and now I will have a banquet in your honor, you who *became lost* and returned to your father's love and *everlasting life!*

ABBA   I-19-09

IN NEED OF A TIME OUT

Is. 28:12
Very well then, with foreign lips and strange tongues God will speak to this people, to whom he said, "This is a resting place, let the weary rest"; and, "This is the place of repose"-- meaning: (Place your trust in Me...)

My child, when mounting pressures assail you (attacked physically or with an argument)---with disappointments and overload to the point of despair; and you cannot *feel anything* and *numbness* comes over you,---you My child are in need of a *time out!*

Find a secluded place---and rest, as did I when I needed time for relaxation and also, to meditate. So it is with you. The cares of this broken world are *legion*

Leave all lines of communication far behind, and get away---even dear one, in your own place of rest or far away. There are so many negative voices or promises made to you that were not fulfilled or were broken---leave that to Me; for I know and see all of each troubled soul. I AM everywhere present.

You are shackled by "time" and circumstances---I AM not! I AM outside of time. I see the beginning and the end of all things. I AM El-Shaddai (Almighty God).

While you are in your earthly flesh, you cannot comprehend. But the day will come when we will see each other face to face, when I will reveal all the wonders of the Galaxies to you.

Be at peace ---be at rest. We will have an eternity together!

ABBA   9-3-09

IN NOTHING BE ANXIOUS

Ps. 139:3
You discern my going out and my lying down; you are familiar with all my ways.

I *have* charted the path ahead of you---and I will tell you when and where to stop and rest!

I AM in all your situations; and I know your strengths and weaknesses, your victories and your failures. Learn to trust Me in all the things you do—in My name!

Start the day with prayer, and dear one, before you leave your bed in the morning---speak to Me as king David did. "O Lord---tell me clearly what to do today and which way to turn."

My son, My daughter---plan for the future but take life a day at a time. It will bring health to your body and keep you from worries that affect your health.

Live in the *forever now*; because you, My child, were created, as was mankind, to live beyond this short earthly life.

You are alien residents in this broken world where Satan the prince of this world brought death through Adam's sin in the Garden of Eden---and sin remains unto this very day!

My Son came to save mankind from sin and restore man to his rightful place with Me!

Practice kingdom living: righteousness, peace and joy in the Holy Spirit. You can and will live above the circumstances of this world!

ABBA   9-12-09

IN THE LAND OF THE LORD

2 Kings 8:1
Now Elisha had said to the woman whose son he had restored to life, "Go away with your family and stay for a while wherever you can, because the Lord has decreed a famine in the land that will last seven years." The woman proceeded to do as the man of God said. She and her family went away and stayed in the land of the Philistines seven years.

In the land of the Lord I will sojourn (live temporarily). In the land of the Lord I will *rest*.

From His mighty hand---I receive His gift of love. In total submission—I allow His strong right arm to enfold Me.

Gently He presses me to his breast---whispering---rest, rest---The battle this day is mine alone---take refuge against My chest.

Who among you will let My heart of hearts provide for your every need? In this time of quietness---In this act of peace, know that your angels surround you---know their release. For from My heart to theirs---orders of paths of glory are checked and underscored; your way was charted the day you chose to be absorbed.

You are that vital part of My body that is equipped to intercede---totally trusting for others in their darkest hour of need.

Go now from My mountain top---go now from the court of the Lord. Pick up your battle garment and--- stand still, for the battle is not yours.

Fill your thoughts on My Fatherhood---dwell upon the Son. My very Spirit will define each act of warfare and let you know when that *battle is won.*

Take up your cross just now---hold it aloft and shout, "Victory---victory is His---my mouth shall speak the praises of the Lord---Let all flesh bless His name!"

ABBA   5-1-89

INTERNAL WICKEDNESS AND DISHONESTY

Matthew 12:25
Jesus knew their thoughts, and said to them, "Every kingdom divided against itself will be ruined, and every city or household divided against itself will not stand."

A word about an *unguarded house* (your inner being): *Stay alert.* Cover it with protective prayer. Day and night the enemy seeks to invade its walls; iniquity and trouble are within it. (Ps. 55:10)

But I have stopped his attempt at invasion--- from attacking your *inner* man after My Son paid it all on that brutal cross.

He has made you free indeed, enjoying all the fruits of His labor, freeing you to give your *will* to Me and allow Me to use you as I will!

Free to serve Me on the mission field of life sharing the hope that is within you, beloved. Suffering the stings of the unsaved, because you do not run after them in the darkest of earthly pleasures!

Though you patrol the walls of the city night and day against invaders, the real problem in the city is *internal* wickedness and dishonesty that is entrenched within common man---those who will not accept Jesus' redemption for everyone! Stay on the alert. Take cover under My protective umbrella.

ABBA

JESUS REVEALS HIS DEATH AND OUR REWARD

Matthew 16:23-26

Jesus turned and said to Peter, "Out of my sight, Satan! You are a stumbling block to me; you do not have in mind the things of God, but the things of men." Then Jesus said to his disciples, "If anyone would come after me, he must deny himself and take up his cross and follow me. For whoever wants to save his life will lose it, but whoever loses his life for me will find it. What good will it be for a man if he gains the whole world, yet forfeits his soul? Or what can a man give in exchange for his soul?

After three years of walking close to Me, Peter could not yet see—with spiritual eyes---who I was, and where I came from: For the Holy Spirit could not come until I was crucified!

My child, can you understand or even imagine the magnitude of what was about to take place?

Peter was presumptuous, and after years of taking charge of any given situation, could not fathom the love of God in allowing His Son to die on a naked cross for mankind; but I knew what sturdy stock he was made of.

My child---are you like Peter, a take charge man or woman, making short or long term decisions at home, at work, and at play? Those dear ones make natural leaders, especially those who have given their *wills* to Me!

The New Testament Church began that day---after the Holy Spirit fell on those who were gathered together in one place on the day of Pentecost---when tongues of fire rested on each one, and they were all *filled* with the Holy Spirit. (Acts. 2:2-4)

From that day---still even today, churches were and are being birthed with those who have cast their lot with My Son Jesus, knowing in their heart of hearts that the Holy Spirit resides in their inner man!

I have given those stalwart ones the *authority* and *power* to do even *greater things* in the salvation of common man (Jn. 14:12) as never before!

The days are short, and it pleases Me to see the young men and women giving over their hearts to Me to do with as I will, sending them into all parts of the world to bring the *good* news to some who have never heard about Jesus, the Christ (Messiah), and kingdom living.

Go and do likewise and receive your reward---the day when I release you to live in the kingdom of heaven.

Blessed children, I honor you--- as you honor Me

ABBA   8-13-09

KEEP CLAIMING YOUR HEALING

1 Cor. 12:9
...to another faith by the same Spirit; to another gifts of healing by that one Spirit.

Child of God---I know you believe, I know love Me. Fear not---come out of confusion and keep claiming your healing, and I will do the rest.

This enemy of ours is an out and out coward, despicable, but still claims this world as his own; but you dear one are not of this world, and you know he has no claim on you.

Woe to him on that day of the all-consuming fire meant especially for him and his followers.

Courage child---courage! Keep claiming that protective wall of healing surrounding your very being.

Be strong, and know that you live and breathe beyond your senses. Keep walking in faith and trust---Keep talking to the who-so-ever-wills in faith and trust.

Continue to be My teaching and mentoring servant to all who grace your path.

ABBA

Luke 7: 20-23
When the men came to Jesus, they said, "John the Baptist sent us to you to ask, 'Are you the one who was to

come, or should we expect someone else?'" At that very time Jesus cured many who had diseases, sicknesses and evil spirits, and gave sight to many who were blind. So he replied to the messengers, "Go back and report to John what you have seen and heard: The blind receive sight, the lame walk, those who have leprosy are cured, the deaf hear, the dead are raised, and the good news is preached to the poor. Blessed is the man who does not fall away on account of me."

KEEP TO THE PATH

Ps. 27:11
Teach me your way, O Lord; and lead me in a straight path...

O! Lord, my heart rejoices as I read Ezekiel's words (Ezek. 36:24-26) " . . .for I will take you from the nations, and gather you from all countries and bring you back into your own land. I will sprinkle clean water on you and you will be clean; I will cleanse you from all your impurities and from all your idols. I will give you a new heart and put a new spirit within you. I will remove from you your heart of stone and give you a heart of flesh."

Yes! I have allowed you to rest on some sand bars along the way; but, dear ones, I have through your cry of repentance brought you into the center of My flowing, on-going river.

Keep to the path—with your spiritual eyes on Me! Look ahead; for I AM bringing My church into the *depths of the river!*

When I bring you to the crest of a wave—look about you, and catch those sitting *high and dry* on a sand bar. Give them a strong nudge back into the *stream of life.*

ABBA

KEEP YOUR EYE ON THE PRIZE

1 Cor. 9:24
Do you not know that in a race all the runners run, but only one gets the prize? Run in such a way as to get the prize.

For the joy that was set before Him (Jesus) He kept His eyes on the finish line! Where do you concentrate your eyes? Are your eyes following the Lord?

He has commissioned every believer around the world to follow Him---in all things. Most certainly I have called every true believer to focus his eyes on the *prize* and to finish the work that I have called you to do.

My son gave up His position in heaven (temporarily) to buy you, a lost soul, back and bring you into a royal position of son-ship!

You are automatically recruited to serve in My army! Jesus said, "Greater things shall you do than I have done; for I Am returning to the Father."

Pause and think about that, loved one! Jesus and the Holy Spirit and I---are the trio in heaven itself. He, Jesus, came to this earth and called all those who now have the same mission He did: to go and seek out those who haven't heard---to come to My father's heart, as you share the *good news* with all the who-so-ever-wills!

All is being made ready. Forget about earth time; for when you *cross over* to the kingdom in heaven---I will have a ready question, "Did you go into all the world to seek and to save?"

Did you share the gift of salvation with your neighbor next door? I admonish you, loved one---keep your eyes on the prize, and cross the line of victory.

95

I want to say to each and every one of you, "Well done good and faithful servant---well done! Enter into the house of your Lord!"

ABBA   9-30-09

KEPT BY THE POWER OF GOD

Psa. 40:1-2
   I waited patiently for the Lord; he turned to me and heard my cry. He lifted me out of the slimy pit, out of the mud and mire; he set my feet on a rock.

O! Child, who struggles with *walking clean* before Me, who so easily stumbles along the path of righteousness, peace, and joy in the Holy Spirit, write these Psalms upon your soul and spirit and you will by-pass the pit-falls of this earth!

   I know that in your heart of hearts you long to stand upright and keep My covenant. Know this: "Your eyes must be continually looking towards Me, your Lord and Savior; and---for my name's sake---know that I always pardon your iniquities when you repent of your misdeeds--- for they are great!

   Stay very close to Me and I will teach you My way, bringing you into a precious state of growing maturity.

   You have put yourself into My care and keeping—and I bless you for it! Like King David of old who said to Me, "Lord---tell me clearly what to do and which way to turn." I never fail to answer your call for you to speak a word of wisdom to those who are weary (Is. 50:4).

   Do this, My child, and I will continually guide you to your desired haven!

ABBA   8-6-02

KEPT IN THE HOLLOW OF HIS HAND

Ps 18:35

You give me your shield of victory, and your right hand sustains me; you stoop down to make me great.

See the vision of My protective hand. See yourself cupped in the hollow of My hand. Yes---dear child, I under gird as you move along. For I place Myself between you and him, who would wound, tear, and kill you if he could!

O how he trembles, when in my hand you place yourself and dwell in the safety of My presence as you walk along. Feel the tingle of My Spirit coursing (running) through you now!

O! You are worthy, little lamb, for He took your place upon that tree---that spotless lamb, "Ancient of Days." (Dan 7:9)

O! How Jesus prays continually for you.

Now in this very hour I can say, "Lord, scatter all my enemies, and put them all to shame; for glory be to God--- You are my guide and stay!"

Rest, rest in My cradle of love; know that your angels keep watch as you rest in My complete protection. Know that you are totally cared for in the flesh as well as in the inner man (spirit).

I transfer you now to My breast as I receive another to be kept in the hollow of My hand.

Now---dear beloved child---I send you back to work for Me on planet earth---for a season, gathering all that I cause to cross over in knowledge and truth of My son Jesus as you minister to their bodily needs and souls.

Go now in your rested extended life to serve Me and mankind. I will guide you along the way, capturing more souls and readying them to enjoy "kingdom living" here on earth.

Preparing them for "kingdom living" with Me as they cross over the vale into My arms; until that day I bring you home---as you finish your assigned service to Me, loved one---for My care and keeping.

ABBA   2-1-11

LET EVERYTHING BE DONE IN ORDER

1 Cor. 14:40
> Everything should be done in a fitting and orderly way.

I AM a God of order, and so all My children should follow suit. Let nothing be done in haste! Carefully plan your work for Me as I guide your mind and hands throughout each day.

Then when all is in order, work your plan. I am not the author of confusion, but of peace, as should be seen in all the churches throughout the world!

This is the order to follow in everything you do. Eons ago, and to this very day, when I open My mouth to speak things into existence, know that it is thoroughly thought through, before I act upon it.

I, who am the "Father of Light," in the very beginning--- after creating the earth---released My Spirit to hover over the face of the waters; then I commanded, "Let there be Light" and there was light (Gen. 1:2).

For an orderly lifestyle read all of Genesis 1—as a perfect pattern of organizing your daily life, whether at home, work or play!

It will bring health to your marrow, and order to all your ways. Pay everything forward; do not look back at yesterday's mistakes, but learn from them!

Live your lives for Me a day at a time in your 'well thought out' master plan. If there is any deviation in those plans, know that I AM outside of time and see the beginning and end of all things. I will make the corrections; trust My guidance---it will keep you on the path toward your ultimate goal, which is *life everlasting* in eternity with Me and your loved ones who have gone on before you, beloved!

ABBA

LET GOD WORK IN YOUR LIFE

Hebrews 13:6

So we say with confidence, "The Lord is my helper; I will not be afraid. What can man do to me?"

Remove all skepticism, and let Me work in your life. Throw all caution to the wind, and rely on naked trust in Me!

This, My child, is what you have to do; for you are a free moral agent, and I cannot do this for you! So reach out in blind faith and do it---you will receive a blessing one hundred fold!

I know the thoughts you think, and I know that you eagerly want and wait for My appearance in all of your circumstances.

David of old---simply said, under My prompting, "Chart the path ahead of me, O lord, and tell me where to stop and rest."

He also said "Since you are my rock and my fortress, for the sake of your name lead and guide me." (Ps 31:3)

If, My child, you memorize these two verses---your days will be filled with anticipation of what events I will bring across your path.

Trust Me completely! I will fill your life full of expectancies that you never imagined could, or would, come to pass in your life!

"Call to me and I will answer you and tell you great and unsearchable things you do not know." (Jer. 33:3)

I AM yours and you are My own, beloveds, and it does not yet appear the things I have for you; things for good and not for evil.

Soak in My love letter to you (Bible); I am preparing you for kingdom living here on earth and in heaven, filled with righteousness, peace, and joy in the Holy Spirit.

I have assigned angels to watch over you night and day. Always be ready to give to others the hope that is within you in your daily talks with the who-so-ever-wills that cross your path.

Stay on the alert; for the devil and his hoards of hell are always looking and waiting for you to *drop your guard*---so they can gain a foot-hold in your life!

Remember---*you are never alone!* I AM just a whisper away---day or night, for I never sleep.

Until that day---when I call you to Myself, remember that you are simply a *resident alien* on the planet earth!

ABBA   7-21-09

100

LET THE CAPTIVES GO FREE

Isa 61:1-2

The Spirit of the Lord is on me, because he has anointed me to preach good news to the poor. He has sent me to proclaim freedom for the prisoners and recovery of sight for the blind, to release the oppressed, to proclaim the year of the Lord's favor.

Respond to the book of life, respond to the body of Christ, respond to Me. Reach out to the people that are close to you---awakening their plight.

Go in person. Go in spirit; help them to turn their darkness into light and intercede for their release and well-being. Satan has bound and seduced them---torn their dignity to shreds.

You can---you must! I through you will release them; go and clean up their pen!

Children of the *new dawn,* children of the day---rise up and move forward; meet me at the *summit* of the mountain, view with Me fallen man.

Reach out your hand, encourage—lift up that wayward man! Their eyes have become weak from a long stay in the darkness.

Help steady their faltering hands, for they see no filth about them---their senses dulled, their ears so *hard of hearing.*

Lend them a hand---unlock their soul and let the brightness of My Son shine in! For at first they do not see Me--- the Almighty one. They are not aware of Me.

O! Stop them from consuming another *pill.*

For I---through you can stir their hearts. I through you can give them that fresh start, that push of encouragement---Yes! Without them knowing it.

Your special love and concern for them have placed them upon My breast; now from that vantage point of power, I will save them in that very hour.

Steady My child---forge ahead---go and show them how to respond to My Son and to the body of Christ---and to Me!

ABBA   7-22-83

LIFE PROVIDES NO SHORT CUTS

James 1:3
...the testing of your faith develops perseverance.

As you walk, work, and speak in My name to all that I cause to cross your path, be open to prepare your daily tasks!

Let Me chart the paths (Ps. 139:3) Do not be in haste to finish your assignment. Check your map (Bible) thoroughly and *don't* pass the instructions that I have for you; for the path I have for you today is *well marked* by My signposts in this turmoil filled world.

Stop at each signpost, and first count the cost that I have charted for you: It is the signs of *patience, perseverance,* and *constant persistence!*

Remember, beloved, that you are in jeopardy if you *don't count the cost.* Do not hurry through this marker. Wait on My Spirit to move in and through your spirit and He will well define your mission, whether the task is large or small.

Have you prayed through the mission's requirements that He has assigned for you? Then ---having done all, stand in readiness, armor in place.

Put on "the sword of the Spirit." Is it shielded and sharp and able to cut through all the hazards along the way? Are your feet shod with the shoes of righteousness? Are you prepared to walk tall in a just and upright manner?

Will your approach in service to Me reveal a virtuous person? Will others sense that you truly are morally right as you engage them?

Do they sense your love and concern for their wellbeing? (Rom. 15:5)

Follow these directions implicitly---with *no short cuts* in your walk through life. I AM with you to guide and protect your way. And the day that I bring you out of this world I will proudly declare, "Well done, good and faithful servant, enter into the kingdom of everlasting life, living in My very presence!

ABBA   9-26-09

Tit. 2:2   1 Tim. 6:11   Luke 8:15

LOOK AFTER EACH OTHER

Hebrews 12:15
See to it that no one misses the grace of God and that no bitter root grows up to cause trouble and defile many.

My children, this verse is a sober warning to everyone, especially concerning the intimacy of a man and his wife.

I have made them to become as one, helpmates to each other! It is so important that two *believers* in My Son become united in their closeness always taking the time to pray and praise Me in accord (mutual agreement); for I inhabit the praises of My children. During your prayer time together, if there is any *root of bitterness* from either the man or his wife---put aside all activities and talk it out.

Satan loves for you to harbor even the slightest root of bitterness; if it is not dealt with immediately---it becomes a giant wall between the two of you.

Quietly discuss the reason for the bitterness between you, with civility, and come to an understanding; then turn to Me, and in obedience, both of you repent and go on with your daily duties.

If you follow my counsel---you will live a victorious life together, and be able to go about your ministries of seeking and speaking to the lost, strayed, or captured by Satan and his fallen angels.

What blessings I will bring to the both of you, and you will sense the peace that passes all understanding --- growing closer to each other and able to find victory whenever the dark one challenges you each day!

Watch and pray daily for each other. Your families and friends will draw close to Me through your example of oneness; those within your sphere of influence will see and know that herein is a force to be reckoned with.

Stay on the alert, and never, never go to bed angry!

ABBA   7-23-09

LORD PURIFY MY HEART

Titus 2:13-14

...we wait for the blessed hope—the glorious appearing of our great God and Savior, Jesus Christ, who gave himself for us to redeem us from all wickedness and to purify for himself a people that are his very own, eager to do what is good.

Lord---purify my heart, and bring me in right relationship with you! Let me serve you with all my heart, each precious day that you allow me to walk this earth and to serve you in this broken world!

Our country is being captured by satanic influence. Our founding fathers created our constitution to allow our citizens, past and present, to live under God, a free nation.

Thousands upon thousands of our military have given up their lives to protect our ability to live in a free society where man should be able to live out his life in perfect peace.

Greed and power of our lawmakers threatens to by-pass man's right to exercise his freedom under our present constitution, threatening to seize our country for their own self- aggrandizement.

O! Lord---we pray that you will forgive our country for its enormous sins against your father's heart. We are repenting and interceding for our beloved nation to come back to its first beginnings.

Our lawmakers---like the Pharisees of old, have become blinded by Satan and with oligarch hearts are living their lives under deception!

O! God in heaven, bring about change in our world. Let your children, under your Son Jesus, be an example of godly living through their unselfish acts of interceding for common man.

My children---know that I care for all of mankind; but for the most part, throughout the ages, My church on earth has not stepped up en masse to become the church doing the work of evangelism letting the few that have a true heart for missions near and far go into all the world to seek and to save the who-so-ever wills for Me!

I have purified your hearts, faithful ones. Now go in My name doing the work of an evangelist, and bring as many as you can to My throne of grace until the day when I will come again to take all who honor My Son to My bosom to live forever in eternity with Me!

ABBA   7-22-09

MAKERS OF PEACE

Romans 14:19
Let us therefore make every effort to do what leads to peace and to mutual edification.

Champions of the fire---champions of the soul---makers of peace---anointed of God. Continue to share My love with others. You are messengers called into the presence of the King.

Shake the dust from off your feet of those who are uncommitted. Do not dwell on the years gone by. Continue to put the past behind you; for I have made you to overcome by the blood of the Lamb.

Makers of peace, your shackles will soon be lifted and placed in the corner for destruction. Now freed for service to the King, lift high the banner of God's anointed.

Makers of peace, bring glory to My name. Makers of peace, ride high the crest of salvation. Strengthen the weak in faith---point them to the mountain made white by the lamb. (Rev. 7:14)

Makers of peace, gather in the spoil. Lift high the banner once more! Grasp the hand of those waiting to be saved. Stay strong---wait on the Lord. Turn the page of tomorrow and see that I continue to reign on the throne of righteousness.

Makers of peace, loyal to the Son---reach out to brighter tomorrows sanctified by the Lamb. Are you weary? Are you sick at heart? Fear not. It is My desire to give you the Kingdom---it is yours!

Placements (sanctuaries) have been anchored along the path, where food abounds. Take and eat---stop and refresh yourself. Take in the sights and the splendor of your surroundings---lights filled with brilliant color. Bask in the radiance of their beauty. Here is a path to be desired, a path in which to grow---a path to fill your heart's desire.

Be in fellowship with the Son; fellowship with the Spirit. Be content within yourself. (It is well with my soul). When you are rested, walk on---walk tall. Listen for the angelic voices, guardians of your soul. You are never alone!

ABBA

MAN IN TROUBLE

Psalm 34:17
    The righteous cry out, and the Lord hears them;
he delivers them from all their troubles.

Man with troubles, cry louder and ponder your soul within. Man with troubles, a portion of your breast at rest---a portion of your breast *at war*.

Who can implore---who can say, "The man next to me is a knave." Get in tune with My Son. Live each day as if it were your last.

Bring honor---bring victory---bring Love. For from My vantage point above---I see each man's motives. I see each man's gains.

I see that men long to bring themselves a touch of fame, a touch of class; even I must harass another made the same. For in My image---man was made to survive!

Man, in *storm tossed waters*, cry louder. Set everything aside and concentrate on Him (Jesus) in life lived in the flesh for now; but give equal time to the Spirit within you. Loose your chains. Give love. Man in trouble and confusion, all you need is your shoes; slip them on and walk the path. Go fishing for man---heap them on My lap!

Do all things starting with prayer, then, be off in spirit, be off in the physical. Let a song on your lips---break forth.

Man in trouble, let your mind be unclouded. The battle still rages on. Need I remind you again? No strange thing is happening, for we war against principalities and the ravages of time!

Man in trouble, cry louder, "Jesus, free me from my sin today, and tomorrow if I live. My desire: to walk within your palatial home on floors of *gold* ---worshipping the Father, worshipping the Son, worshipping the Holy Spirit---*blessed three in one."*

ABBA

MAN'S INHUMANITY TO MAN

Psalm 118:8
It is better to take refuge in the Lord than to trust in man. It is better to take refuge in the Lord than to trust in princes.

Recent events shake you to the core . . .

My children, will you never learn that apart from Me---man in the depth of his being inherited the very nature of disobedience since the fall!

My son kept His silence, at times, about himself and the mission I sent Him on, for he knew the hearts of man.*

He spoke in parables, but to His elect He said, "It is given to you to know the mysteries of the kingdom of heaven, but to them it is *not given.* " (Mt. 13: 10-11)

And now, loved one, ---I speak to man's inhumanity to man as it has touched you. Man's greed, his struggle for power, whether at the national or local level, to service his natural desires and affections has come against you as a resistant fortified wall.

Now We come to you. To you who have been wronged I say: Don't be overcome by evil. Overcome evil by your actions and witness.

I have not left you without tools to fight. Come before Me with praise. Come before Me with prayer. Put on your protective armor, and *stand.*

You have no need to take physical action. You *do need* to stand and watch how I work for you. For the battle, loved ones, is not yours but mine. (2 Chron. 20:15-17)

Show them by words and deeds that you serve the Living God. This is a hard saying to you who have suffered much at the hands of your oppressors.

To you who in the natural man would repay evil by your own might, *don't!* It only leads to illness and death. The death I speak of is *carrying on in your chosen course.* Win or lose, it is not My way of dealing.

Follow Me now as I rebuild your broken hearts. *Follow Me!* Soak in My Word. Plumb its depths; and as you do so, I will lift you above this broken world into the joy of the Lord!

When you do this, beloveds, others will be drawn to you as a thirsty soul is drawn to refreshing waters. Join with Me now. Together we are the wellsprings of life to a frightened and fear-driven world. Freely give them to drink.

Selah (Pause and think of *all the above*)!

Jn. 2: 24-25
But Jesus would not entrust himself to them, for he knew all men. He did not need man's testimony about man, for he knew what was in a man.

1 Peter 3:14-17
"Do not fear what they fear; do not be frightened." But in your hearts set apart Christ as Lord.

MARVELS OF THE UNIVERSE

Job 9:8-10
He alone stretches out the heavens and treads on the waves of the sea. He is the Maker of the Bear and Orion, the Pleiades and the constellations of the south. He performs wonders that cannot be fathomed, miracles that cannot be numbered.

Could you not know? Could you not see? Could you not hear the marvels that await you just ahead, My beloved child?

The eye has not yet seen what is ahead of you---a kingdom filled with the joy of angelic music and constant praises to My Name!

Hidden wonders—now kept from you until you cross to the *other side*.

An eternity without pain and suffering; for there is nothing broken in My heavenly kingdom. Ageless you will be. An eternity to enjoy the presence of family and friends who have gone on before you!

And an eternity to expand your senses as you see Me, praising Me up close, and the biblical saints whom I used to write down eternal messages in My *Living Word.*

This and more awaits you beloved, this and so much more!

ABBA   6-16-10

MINISTRY OF COMPASSION

2 Chron. 36:15
The LORD, the God of their fathers, sent word to them through his messengers again and again, because he had pity on his people and on his dwelling place.

Who will go? Who will stay? Who will say: "You are loved, we care, we will share, and we will pray. We will seek God, even in tears, to aid your release from bondage."

So many--- there are so many that cannot find the *door.* "There are no handles," they say. "How are we to know the way?" Deluded ones out for fun. Deluded ones taking up the gun. If they only knew how thin the thread is that holds it all together.

A violent windstorm---a rumble in the sea will bring them to their knees. Dullness of hearing within My camp (church) stifles the chant that could bring about change.

Your mission call still rings true. Your mission is soon coming---out of the blue. So many valleys are along a narrow way. No vehicle can travel there without despair.

But enough, I say, enough. My own are tough and strong in spirit. My children are rough, even to the shaking of the soul and spirit of those too lame to call out for help; but help is on the way.

Seek out---seek out by prayer and praise---others like you who will take up the fray and pray forth a blessing so big, so bold that it will bring them into the fold!

ABBA

MIRROR MY FATHER

John 8:38-44
I am telling you what I have seen in the Father's presence, and you do what you have heard from your father....the devil.

John 14:24
He who does not love me will not obey my teaching. These words you hear are not my own; they belong to the Father who sent me.

You are My *leaven and poured out wine.* I cause people to be drawn to you. *Mirror My Son* as you work among those fear-ridden and often-time frightened souls. As you speak and pray---as you counsel in My name—you will have moved them closer to My throne.

In so doing---you may hear the *dark voice* say, "Physician---heal yourself." (Lu. 4:23) And again---"he has helped others---but help does not come his way."

Fear not, little one. I do not delay your *own renewal.* For it is My good pleasure to give good gifts to My own. Carry on in the shadow of My extended right arm. I continue to use you, as I will!

You have, with Me, fought many battles with the enemy, and yet not a hair on your head has been singed by his flames of fire and distortion while trying to attack you from all sides.

But as long as you are wearing (spiritually) Jesus' seamless garment, the enemy cannot penetrate your defenses!

Carry on the work that you do daily to advance the kingdom on earth as it is in heaven. Continue---in your small groups to read, pray, and praise My name.

That is where deep connection is found in the bond of brotherly and sisterly love---uniting in love for the cause of Christ.

ABBA   11-17-81

Matthew 18:19-20

Again I tell you, that if two of you on earth agree about anything you ask for, it will be done for you by my Father in heaven. For where two or three come together in my name, there am I with them.

MISSIONARY PREPAREDNESS

Isaiah 40:3

A voice of one calling: "In the desert prepare the way for the Lord; make straight in the wilderness a highway for our God..."

Patterns and pictures match when aligned. Sense the nobleness of the task set before you. When, in My wisdom, through you, you sense a definite pattern of living for or against Me, notice how they act.

Study their way of life. Some are striving for perfection, knowing in their heart of hearts, that it is unobtainable--- but they rush on in endless pursuit of it. Or they may say one thing, but in actuality their words do not line up with their actions!

Match their efforts with the reflection (image) of Jesus. Show them, by comparison, that I fit all their needs and desires and am their ultimate sanctuary.

They try so hard to measure up to man's image of man---not to My image of man, which is, "Christ in you, the hope of glory."
(Col. 1:27)

I will lead you in what to say---when to say it---and how much to say! Love them---practice patience with them. Their shyness is a cover-up to keep from being trampled on. Some are learning but have never come to the knowledge of the truth. But you are learning to keep going; I am with you to the end!

ABBA

1 Peter 3:15

But in your hearts set apart Christ as Lord. Always be prepared to give an answer to everyone who asks you to give the reason for the hope that you have.

MY INVITATION TO THE WORLD

Is. 55:1-2

Come, all you who are thirsty, come to the waters; and you who have no money, come, buy and eat! Come, buy wine and milk without money and without cost. Why spend money on what is not bread, and your labor on what does not satisfy? Listen, listen to me and eat what is good, and your soul will delight in the richest of fare.

I said that I would make an everlasting covenant with you. O! Listen that you may live. Don't waste your time and efforts for that which will quickly fade away; but concentrate on the things that are everlasting and time will not destroy them!

The spine tingling things that appeal to your senses will so soon fade away and leave you hungering and thirsting for *everlasting things*!

My 'call' is for you to serve your fellow man in his everyday needs and to strengthen his hold on life everlasting.

Spend quality time devouring My words of life, and why I sent My Son to bring My wayward children back into the fold!

When you weigh the fleeting pleasure, and days allotted to mankind, against eternity with Me and your loved ones who have gone on before you, you can readily see that the balance is tipped towards kingdom living, here now on earth, and then when I call you home, throughout all eternity.

Things that are waiting for My children---as they see Me now in an imperfect world---then face to face in heaven's light, they can now only imagine.

O! Be that one who will take on the joy-filled task of introducing Me to all the who-so-ever-wills that are now living in darkness. Bring them, O! Bring them into My presence!

ABBA   10-26-09

MY PLANS FOR YOU NEVER FAIL

Jer. 29:11

"For I know the plans I have for you, declares the LORD," plans to prosper you and not to harm you, plans to give you hope and a future.

Shades of gold---shades of yellow---can you distinguish between the two?

Try, if you can, to see the light---to see that I AM right in all that I do.

Though you may not know---though you cannot understand---My plans for you never change. I match minds; I match times.   Suffice it to say, about those wayward ones who cause you discomfort, bite your tongue and bide your time. Spend it in intercessory prayer for that discontented one.

Watch the circumstances as I bring them into alignment with My Word!

Watch them as they begin to mend their ways.   You mean a lot to them; you are all they've got.

What is time? ----It doesn't matter.   What was said to them in love will bear fruit for good, and not for evil! Continue to pray and praise Me more; continue on as I redeem the time, as I even the score.

Be on your way to others in need of comfort and your prayers. Remember---We conquer together!

ABBA   5-1-83

MY SALVATION IS INCREASED IN YOU

Psalm 25:4-5
Show me your ways, O LORD, teach me your paths; guide me in your truth and teach me, for you are God my Savior, and my hope is in you all day long.

This, dear ones, comes from *soaking* in the word. Spend quality time in slowly ingesting every word; you will notice as you read through the psalms that I end some messages

116

with the Hebrew word, *Selah*, which simply means: pause think about what you have read; let it soak into your inner man!

For I want you to come to know the *deeper* things that I have reserved for My dedicated followers, just as I shared them with My twelve apostles.

As you become more and more aware of My secrets as they are unfolded to you, you will be better equipped to reach out to the *new babes* in Me.

Share My heart of hearts with all of those dear saints who are willing to pay the price of My love letters from home and receive a taste of kingdom living while in their bodily forms!

Become soldiers in My army, with the authority and power given you at, *any time*, to do and help finish the work that I came to do.

Yes! Greater things shall you do, dear beloved of father God, for there still remains much work to do for Me in the *ingathering* of new saints into My kingdom.

So---O! Resident aliens---until I return and bring you home to find rest on My bosom, continue on in your search for all the who-so-ever-wills who eagerly look to know Me--- through you---as I bring them across your path and stop at your *watering hole* (home), and they learn from you how to rest in My salvation and increase in knowledge and wisdom---as have you!

ABBA   8-19-09

NAME ABOVE ALL NAMES

Exodus 3:14-15
And God said to Moses, "I am who I am. This is what you are to say to the Israelites: 'I AM has sent

me to you.'" God also said to Moses, "Say to the Israelites, 'The LORD, the God of your fathers— the God of Abraham, the God of Isaac and the God of Jacob—has sent me to you.' This is my name forever, the name by which I am to be remembered from generation to generation...."

I am El Shadai (God Almighty) the Lord and Master of all things. I AM above and beyond time. I hold all the galaxies in My hands. Do you---can you---even cope with the enormity of My being?

Yet I made myself lower than the angels to rescue common man from the grasp of him who once was so close to My heart---but like Judas who betrayed Me, he decided to become the god of all things created.

Yes! He was a creature of beauty and a site to behold, who convinced the very angels who surrounded him that he would be like Me and claimed many followers.

So I consigned him to perdition, along with his followers and named him the "god of this world" to rule and reign *for a time* on earth. He is the father of lies. (Jn. 8:44)

From Adam to this very day all who pay him allegiance and are filled with his spirit and practice his inhumanity to man and grievous sins will be lost if they do not turn to My Son.

We three (counseled together) and My son agreed to come to earth as common man and suffer for all of My created children, to die for the sins of mankind, and to rebuild the bridge back to My father's heart.

Those who have given Me their *will* and will serve in My army on earth to seek and to save, in *"Jesus' name,* all those who are willing to accept Him as their savior will join the multitude of believers who have gone on before them, uniting, forever, with their family and friends!

118

I caution you this day to let loose of earthly trinkets and to read, pray, and praise Me all the days of your life.

I will reward you by showing you the hidden and fenced in things of this world, filling your lives above and beyond your wildest dreams.

Stay in *obedience* and a lifestyle of repentance--- and sin will not have its way with you!

ABBA

NATURAL MAN AND SPIRITUAL MAN

1 Cor 2: 14
The man without the Spirit does not accept the things that come from the Spirit of God, for they are foolishness to him, and he cannot understand them, because they are spiritually discerned.

The natural man has no idea of heavenly matters for they are spiritually discerned, even the microscopic world.

I have given creative man the ability to invent the most in-depth, complicated items that just a few generations ago were thought to be impossible!

Yet---they pale in comparison to the hidden and deep things of My creative Mind!

Only the Holy Spirit knows the depth of My creativeness. But from the very start of the new dispensation My children can now know the things and thoughts that I have for you, thoughts for good and not for evil, to those for whom My Son died, and who have given over to Me their *wills*. The Spirit-filled man can begin to know the *deeper things* that lay before mankind!

I reward those persistent children who seek to know the deeper things and spend the time delving into the

119

scriptures. I open their eyes to begin to understand *Kingdom living*, reserved for them in heaven and on earth---as they work hand in hand with My Spirit and guiding angels.

O the things I want to reveal to them---I reveal them one at a time. Until I decide to call a halt to this present world!

My prime assignment: "Rescue common man," teach them the Word, in depth, and go into all the world preaching all that the scriptures reveal about My Son and what He came to do.

"Redeem man from Satan's grasp"---as many as time allows, bringing them one by one into the *sheepfold*. I have commissioned my followers to go into all the world to rescue common man from the hold of Satan's demonic forces.

That, My child, for each of you who bear My Name, is what must be uppermost in your thoughts and prayers!

Live a life of incredible love for mankind, and you will draw people to you that can see the way you live. They will discover your heaven-sent peace and tranquility in this corrupt despicable fallen world and perhaps seek to understand.

Live above your circumstances with true faith and trust, along with patience and persistence; and like the pied piper of lore, you will draw many to you like the pull of a powerful magnet---as you live your life for Me in true obedience and a lifestyle of repentance!

Stay on the alert, for the enemy looks for any sign of weakness to drive you off the path toward My heavenly home!

ABBA   7-15-09

NATURE'S BEST

Gen. 2:15
The Lord God took the man and put him in the Garden of Eden to work it and take care of it.

I have placed in the heart of man, the ability to think, to reason, to explore all of nature's *healing wonders* within the crust of the earth.

First, in that garden I created perfect man. You know the rest—how Adam was privy to all that was needed to sustain life, and more!

Then, after the *fall,* the knowledge and wisdom to maintain his health in this broken world was given him to be developed and used for common Man.

Some, in spite of the *fall,* developed their ability to explore resources for health, maintenance, energy and all. Even to this day, your days upon earth, man has the materials to sustain and enjoy the gifts of My love for him!

Yet man in his god-like abilities designed and continues to design and bring forth *artificial substitutes* for *nature's best* with all of their *harmful* side effects, in his own attempt to maintain his health and equilibrium.

These substitutes, which are but *temporary fixes* have, in the long run, been used and abused with disastrous results.

I speak plainly of the use of some manmade *wonder drugs* that capture and destroy My created Man!

To you who have followed *natural* herbs, share them with common man to heal, to allay stress, and to bring comfort and health back into man's very being!

To you who now make use of My *nature's best,* now exposed to their benefits, I charter you to share with one and all.

Why do I do this through you? Especially you who have lovingly given your *Will* to Me in *Servitude?* To use the knowledge to bring the saved and unsaved to My throne of grace.

There is no other purpose than the use of these God-given gifts to regenerate man's inner man—for the most part lying dormant—waiting for release to serve Me without restraint. You have the freedom to *seek* and to help save the lost and *fear-ridden* children of their King!

Need I say more? Though you may be ridiculed by some as you experience in your own body and spirit My *nature's best*, remember: a person with an experience to be healed with natural elements---or by My *miraculous touch*---is never at the mercy of one with an argument.

Go—armor in place and intact. Conquer in My name. Keep your perspective. The cure for all of Man's ills—physical or spiritual---is in the knowledge and recognition of all that I AM!

ABBA   9-8-83

Editor's note: The writer prior to this date was not interested in "natural medicine" but after receiving this word in 1983 and then facing the illness of his wife, diagnosed with cancer in 1999, began to study.

NATURE'S WAY WITHOUT HELP

Psalms 8:1, 3-4

O LORD, our Lord, how majestic is your name in all the earth!... When I consider your heavens, the work of your fingers, the moon and the stars, which you have set in place, what is man that you are mindful of him, the son of man that you care for him?

How futile your efforts to swim against the tide. Follow the systematic way of nature's production; for I have ordered forth all of creation with My common plan for everything under the sun.

The earth revolves around the sun in its selected orbit and I keep all the stars in My numerous galaxies in their own places, everything done decently and in order!

A seed is planted, and in its proper season it breaks through its little shell and grows to its intended height--- from the mighty Oak to that which you cannot see in the microscopic world, to the trillions of cells in your body which, when following My design--- are restored daily!

Thus the seed--- in My timing--- bursts up from the soil and reveals its beauty for all mankind to see, admire, and enjoy. It is one of hundreds of varieties of many trees and plants that brings forth its fruit in its correct season, to be used for the benefit of My created beings.

Most of the natural medicines are brought into the light of day and used by naturopaths to aid common man without the help of scientists' formulations which are accompanied by serious side effects, and which if ingested, bring imbalance to one's system, even at times *death!*

The scientists may copy Me with their inventions, but they will never come close in design or usage.

O! I encourage you to follow nature's way in your daily lives. Never rush into any project without asking those closest to you for prayer or guidance.

I AM as close as your prayer life and praises, for I inhabit the praises of My children!

ABBA   9-26-09

NEGLECTFUL CHILDREN

Matthew 7:26
But everyone who hears these words of mine and does not put them into practice is like a foolish man who built his house on sand.

Neglectful children---who are so asleep---so lazy and disobedient that they are on the very tip of My tongue to spit them out! "Wake up," I say, wake up to that heavenly call to be your brothers' and sisters' keeper!

They need your loving compassion, but you are so bound in your own pursuits that their silent cries for help go unnoticed. You see them---*but not really.*

Your inner man is undernourished, as you fail to get into the Word and *soak* in all of its heavenly dimensions.

Your life races at a whirlwind pace---doing that '*important work.*' But---it is *winter grass* choked full of weeds, so soon to lie dormant.

O why will you die? When you turn to Me again---I will pardon. I will re-commission. Strap on your *winged shoes*; I will take you high above the frenzy.

There your assignments will be clearly shown to you. Wait on Me. Quiet yourselves as you listen to My still small voice *shouting* into your ears: "This, this is the way, walk you in it" "Strap on your armor"---I will protect your flanks. In the meantime, surround your shepherds with the shield of faith; always be ready to quench the fiery darts of the wicked.

We are at war, dear children. We are at war! The heavenly on-going battle has *touched down* among the elite, the misinformed, and those totally given over to Satan himself.

Cry victory. Cry victory, My children, for it is ours. Drive the enemy towards that bottomless pit reserved for

Lucifer and his fallen angels and those who dare, with arrogance, to imitate Me.

Walk tall within My flame of protection---you are Mine!

ABBA

NEW BEGINNINGS—NEW CHALLENGES

Hebrews 12:1
Therefore, since we are surrounded by such a great cloud of witnesses, let us throw off everything that hinders and the sin that so easily entangles, and let us run with perseverance the race marked out for us.

Life for My committed children---those *sold-out* to My perfect *will* for their lives, is a life filled with new beginnings and new challenges. In short---a life lived in a state of repentance.

Remember, committed one, you live in *enemy territory* full of pot-holes---that, if you are not on constant alert, will cause you to stumble and become entangled.

Be of good cheer, I have overcome these entanglements. I---only I---My Spirit actively residing within you, lead and guide you through the entanglements!

You are no longer your own. Try as you might--- without being encased in your holy armor, you are no match for the father of lies. I remind you again: in this world of suffering, whether physical or spiritual, you will have tribulation. "But take heart! I have overcome the world." (Jn.16:33)

Take no thought for your life, but to serve Me well. Live a full victorious life within the confines of this world's tragedies---a life filled with expectations. Keep your eyes on me, *"the author and perfecter"* of your faith. (Heb.12: 2- 6)

Continue, loved one, to pour over this chapter; it is for you and all the who-so-ever-wills---the babes and those walking along the path toward maturity---to live your life in a state of repentance!

Now from this vantage point, loved one, *follow Me* and do the *greater works* that I have committed to your care and keeping.

"I tell you the truth, anyone who has faith in me will do what I have been doing. He will do even greater things than these, because I am going to the Father." (John 14:12)

ABBA

NIGHTLY TEARS-JOY FILLED MORNINGS

Psalm 84:5
   Blessed are those whose strength is in you, who have set their hearts on pilgrimage.

Come into My tent of weeping---for tonight we weep!
Come into My tent of weeping---for it is time, once again, to cry. Take off your shoes My child---kneel and pray; and say to those who are in a state of prayer: "Tonight we weep together."

Do I require all to sit in sackcloth and ashes? No-No-No! In the name of My Son, with all He has done---it is enough---it is enough to come aside and weep. Weep for shame of broken promises---weep for shame of un-accomplished tasks.

Why are you so careless in your appearance, habits, work, ---all in disarray? Think on this---and you will come to the realization that I *do not* have your inner ear nor your inner eye to hear and see Me in all your circumstances.

Return to your first love (Rev. 2:4-5) or I will remove your candlestick out of its place---except you repent! It is a fearful thing to fall into the hands of the living God! (Heb.10:31)

Weep for those who are in pain; weep for those who are unashamed and insensitive to My call---then---when you stand in repentance---*listen*---*listen* for My command! It will surely be given to you!

Now---quiet yourselves. Seek the pages of the book for comfort and guidance. Seek Me in the early morning hours, and you will surely find your mornings filled with Joy.*

Put a song in your heart, and a spring in your step. Praise me in the morning, seek Me in the evening. You will soon see My countenance mirrored in your *own reflection!*

O Love child of Mine, stir up the gifts that are within you. (2 Tim. 1:6) Seek and you shall find (Mt.7:7) Knock and heaven's gate will open. Light from My heavenly throne and Myriads of angels will enthusiastically approve, comfort, and protect you---with anticipation of your *home-coming*---readying the trumpets to herald your arrival---to your joy-filled home!

ABBA   1-14-83

*Rom. 15:13

May the God of hope fill you with all joy and peace as you trust in him, so that you may overflow with hope by the power of the Holy Spirit.

NO REAL UNDERSTANDING

Matthew 13:19

When anyone hears the message about the kingdom and does not understand it, the evil one comes and snatches away what was sown in their heart. This is the seed sown along the path.

Year after year---time after time---immature children with carnal knowledge but no real grasp of the *mission call* play games with their silly intellects. Professing to be wise, their speech and actions betray them.

In the deep recesses of their being, down deep in a self made lock-box, when giving themselves an honest appraisal, they realize their limitations *but will not give up.*

They walk in their own strength---with their own intellectual opinion of themselves, as was Jacob's way of doing things before he wrestled with an angel and was renamed Israel. (Gen. 32:24-28)

Common man says, "I will come up with another plan. God has given me the ability to think through any problem or circumstance very carefully; then I can help all mankind!"

Again the 'but;'---fast or slow reality sets in along with deep-seated doubts. Within the closet of their inner being, in honesty, with quiet introspection---they know their own *short-comings* when not looking to Father God for His help or guidance.

I tell you, My child, "It is *always* the time to run the race toward finishing the course." Tell them by word and deed to pay attention to the rules, (My Word) block out the aggressor, side step the tempter. Don't run here---don't run there. Stand---sing--- shout!

Speak the name above all names. His name, spoken in triumph, crushes and tears down the enemy's strongholds. Lifts and heals the broken hearted. Restores the breach---

conquers all evil, and lays waste those in opposition to the Christ.... "The Holy One of Israel."

ABBA

Psalm 32:9
Do not be like the horse or the mule, which have no understanding but must be controlled by bit and bridle or they will not come to you.

Jeremiah 4:22
My people are fools; they do not know me. They are senseless children; they have no understanding. They are skilled in doing evil; they know not how to do good.

NO SMALL STEP

Proverbs 16:3
Commit to the LORD whatever you do, and your plans will succeed.

You have, by your *will*, submitted your life to Me, your Lord and your master; *no small step!* You have, with the help of My Spirit, bridged the gap between Satan's world, and spirit-filled living.
Now launch out with determination to *read, praise,* and *pray.* Honor Me in all the things that you do in service to Me!
Fill your life with other *committed followers of the way.* When you slip off My path of obedience, repent quickly, and move on; by this act of contrition, you are restored and forgiven. Take this leap of faith and reap the harvest to follow, My beloved one!

ABBA   11-14-81

NOTE THE UPRIGHT MAN

Psalm 37:37
Consider the blameless, observe the upright;
there is a future for the man of peace.

Would you attain to celestial heights? Know that God's
way *up is down!*

Ponder His light, His power, His might as you read His
anointed Word. What price glory? What price fame? You
need to revel in My Glory. Fame is a fleeting *antagonistic*
(unfriendly) way that drains the energy of every man and
woman who puts personal glory over their dedication to
Me.

Yes, I bring fame to all who can correctly and humbly
handle it. For true fame is to walk in My ways, meditate on
My word, and sense the breath of the Holy Spirit's whisper:
"This---this is the way, walk you in it." (Is. 30:21)

Follow the path to the cross. See God's heart and mind
revealed there. Are you able to draw near? Are you able to
feel His pain? What does it take in this broken world to
know His love through His *blood-bought* sacrifice on your
behalf?

It takes reaching out with that weak, withered hand, time
and time again, when you fall; but glory be: the upright
man or woman knows that *quick repentance* brings peace
to a troubled heart!

The sick begged Jesus to let the them to*uch even the
hem of His garment,* and all who did were healed; for My
child, healing comes by *faith,* in the power of His name; the
name above all other names! (Mt. 14:36)

Be instant in prayer---sing His praises. Heavenly
chimes ring out as prayer and praise rise---in His honor!
Show by word and deed the measures of His love in you.

Every thing you say or do should be done in the name of the Lord Jesus, giving thanks to God the Father---through Him. (Col. 3:17)

ABBA

NOTHING TOO HARD FOR GOD

Jer. 32:27
    I am the LORD, the God of all mankind. Is anything too hard for me?

You, O Lord, have shown loving kindness to hundreds of thousands of Your children. The Lord of Hosts is Your name!
    Wonder of wonders---You are *pure love*, and unlike common man---there is no deceit in You. Your heavenly light is cast upon all of mankind.
    You detest the evil that is in renewed man (spiritually reborn) and those who have yet to receive Your son Jesus as their lord and savior.
    For You are no respecter of persons, and treat common man accordingly. You have commissioned us who love and serve Jesus to obey His commandment to go into all the world to seek out and save ---in Your name---those who have never heard or read Your word.
    We have come to know that nothing is too difficult for You. We who are finite man tend to *push back* the seemingly impossible situations that we run into in our quest for the unsaved.
    But when You remind us of the *authority* and *power* that You have given us to bring in those outside of Your family, we in faith and believing trust become more than conquerors in you name.

131

You have told us not to be concerned with just the right words to say; but in our hour of need, you, O! Holy Spirit, will give us the right words to say to those earnestly seeking You (the who-so-ever- wills) and even the greatest of unbelievers; for nothing is too hard for You!

ABBA   8-21-09

OCCUPY TILL I COME

Luke 19:13
...So he called ten of his servants and gave them ten minas. 'Put this money to work,' he said, 'until I come back.'

Do you have any idea of the full magnitude of this message, loved one?

Neither storm, nor strife---persecution or your own failures, at times, will deter you from any mission I send you on!

Even in the heat of the most satanic attack that the enemy can muster against you, I will keep you within My comforting arms!

It is to you, O! Faithful one, that I give the greatest honor; one, who, in spite of physical or spiritual pain, keeps looking to Me, the author and finisher of your faith.

O! Loyal one, I fill you with heavenly strength to walk the walk, and talk the talk: a 'pied piper' of Kingdom living—drawing common man onto My path toward eternal life.

You are well aware of Satan's torturous words sent your way at every turn in the road; but I defeated him on the cross and rose again—leaving you in the hands of the Holy Spirit

---whose brilliant light, brightly shining in front of you, guides and comforts you through the traps and mine fields to constant victory.

For you stand heads and shoulders above the crowd as a lighted being; engraved on your chest are the words, "This is the way—walk you in it."

ABBA   3-3-10

OFFENDERS WILL BE PUNISHED

Mark 9:42
And if anyone causes one of these little ones who believe in me to sin, it would be better for him to be thrown into the sea with a large millstone tied around his neck.

You may say this is a hard saying---but I tell you plainly--- if any one, Christian (so called) or non believer, tempts any new *babe* in Me and thus (by any means) derails them from the path of righteousness, peace, and joy in the Holy Spirit ---*beware*"!

I AM known as "the hound of heaven" and they will wish---before I am through with them, that they were covered with rocks to get away from the consequences that follow!

They should look deep into their inner man and think about what may befall them. I say to them, "Follow your friend who has chosen to give his or her life to Me, and you will soon see the error of your ways. Take a serious look at the lives I died and rose again to redeem---in order to bring all who would follow Me into a life lit by the Light of heaven, who will also guide *you* into joyous living.

Realize that the life you now lead is just a moment *in time*, as you count time, and be saved by the blood shed for you on the cross of Calvary.

And then enjoy a life filled with joyous service in My army of believers, who have faced the enemy (Satan), dressed and fitted in battle gear and then told by Me, "Stop---put down your sword---you need not fight in this battle. Stand, therefore, and watch Me; for the battle is mine---and mine alone!"

Rest now from your futile struggle to obtain all that the world can offer only to die and leave all your worldly possessions for someone else!

Where then is your victory---O! Man of sorrow and defeat!

ABBA   8-18-09

ON THE BASIS OF FAITH IN HIS NAME

Acts 3:16

By faith in the name of Jesus, this man whom you see and know was made strong. It is Jesus' name and the faith that comes through him that has given this complete healing to him, as you can all see.

If My child, you have read this whole chapter---you will notice that Peter, full of faith and trust in My word, having received from My hand au*thority* and *power* had but to utter, "walk;" and the man was immediately healed of his malady.

The man on the receiving end of this command believed *in faith* that he would receive the healing pronounced by Peter!

To this very day, dearest believer, you have the same *power* and *authority* to conquer any malady or pressures from this wicked perverse world...and to accomplish anything in My Name for good and not for evil pursuits...as long as you remain obedient to Me and live a lifestyle of repentance.

On the basis of faith in My name go forth in ministry to the *call* on your life---to seek out and to save in the name of My Son---all whom you come across in your daily life.

Be bold---but not obnoxious, patient without being *pushy*, persistent---but not overbearing; and, loved one, they will catch an aroma about you, sensing that you are motivated by Me.

As a true compassionate, minister for Me, on the basis of *faith in My name*, pray silently for the one who slanderers you ---speaking untruths about you.

Nothing escapes My eyes or ears. Times of refreshment will come from My presence; for I am constantly by your side!

Believe it My child ---Believe it!

ABBA   8-12-09

OPEN PRAYERS SENT MY WAY

Philip. 1:6
   ...Being confident of this, that he who began a
good work in you will carry it on to completion
until the day of Christ Jesus.

Remember---Open prayers sent My way are like a dangling string needing closure!

The string is a series of events; some are short in nature---while others are--- long, limp, and weather-beaten.

I---only I, bring closure to these events My way.

135

I am the one who takes the two ends and fashions them together into one continuous circle from whence the events are co-mingled and flow together becoming one in harmony with the circle of *life eternal*---no beginning and *no ending!*

There in that circle I bring completion, harmony, and peace.

So, dear child, send your string of concerns to Me. I, and only I, can---and will diffuse them, bringing about the greater good; for all things do work together for good to those who love Me.

ABBA

OUR GOD IS A CONSUMING FIRE

Hebrews 12:28-29

Wherefore, since we are receiving a kingdom that cannot be shaken, let us be thankful, and so worship God acceptably with reverence and awe, for our God is a consuming fire.

I have striven with man these many years---and what has he learned since Adam and Eve were driven from My perfect garden? They lusted after that which I told them not to eat: the fruit of the tree of knowledge of good and evil. I told them plainly, "You shall not eat of it; for the day that you eat of it--- you shall surely die!" (Gen. 2:17)

Since that dreadful day---all mankind has run after the world's pleasures, with no thought of Me, their maker and redeemer.

Only those who have accepted the total price I paid on the cross for their sins by shedding My blood for all sinners---those who been brought back into *right relationship* with the father---can walk with Me in that *spiritual garden* in perfect fellowship with Me and will live forever in eternity with Me!

Those who will not give Me their will *willingly,* but choose to live without My guidance through earth's *minefields,* will on their departure from planet earth---suffer eternally in My *consuming fire!*

I, through My servants, go about My business daily--- sharing the *good news* and promise of eternal life with Me; but some still reject My son Jesus as lord and savior. I tell you, loved ones, they are without excuse for the fate that awaits them!

ABBA   7-22-09

OUR GOD WORKS FOR US

Isa. 64:4
Since ancient times no one has heard, no ear has perceived, no eye has seen any God besides you, who acts on behalf of those who wait for him.

Are you---even now---waiting for Me to work out your spiritual and earthly problems?

I can, and will, *if you wait in faith* and trust in My timing. There are many hundreds and thousands who are waiting, as do you, for My intervention in earthly concerns.

For I AM able in an instant to handle them even when the heavenly basket is *full to overflowing!*

I remind all who read this message today that I AM never too late nor too early, but I AM always on time!

My children, live in obedience to My promises and live a lifestyle of repentance. I will answer!

Come to Me all you who are weary and heavy laden and I will give you rest---from you labors. (Mt. 11:28) So come to Me, beloveds, and let your lives be used as an instrument of righteousness (The highest standard of morality)....for all the who-so-ever-wills who come across your path!

ABBA   10-25-09

OUT OF THE DEPTHS OF OUR POVERTY

Luke 15:14
After he had spent everything, there was a severe famine in that whole country, and he began to be in need.

Out of the depths of our poverty we cry out; "O Lord we are weighted down with sin and deprivation. We are at the bottom of a deep chasm, smothered by all manner of refuse, which has so easily consumed us!

Yes, we are responsible for our sins and selfish living, but where is the watchman's call? Where is that constant call to repentance and holy sensitivity to the work of the Lord?

The call is clear when we are standing on the mountain top, the Lord's plans clearly seen---but in the valley, where the heart of the problems exist---ah--- there it is not so easily defined when we allow contrary winds to blur our vision, testing our hold on God Himself.

There when the eye and the ear does not stay focused on the Father's gifts and His son's redemption and eternal promises, the obscurity sets in with arthritic stiffness and dullness.

Lord, there is mercy within the depths of our *poverty*. We remember the *'former and latter days'* of grace. We are keenly aware of Your forbearance. We ask for and receive, by Your mercy and grace, a lifting of the refuse upon us put there by our own hand.

We arise out of the dust and once again accept Your extended hand of love and forgiveness. How often You have set us upon our feet and pointed us in the direction of Your call!

You are by the grace of My command---soldiers, warriors and ambassadors of the King. To strengthen your armor, take the sword of the Spirit and cut a clean pathway to long unattended roads---which lead to the Heart of God.

The trumpet has blown. Sound the alarm---bring along the who-so-ever- wills.

ABBA

Eph. 6:17
Take the helmet of salvation and the sword of the Spirit, which is the word of God.

OUT WITH THE OLD

1 Cor. 5:7
Get rid of the old yeast that you may be a new batch without yeast--as you really are. For Christ, our Passover lamb, has been sacrificed.

Tread the winepress---make the circle complete. Tread the winepress and stay on your feet. Co-laborers together--- now the message is complete.

Stretch your faith---stretch it far. Some are masters at misunderstanding---masters of deceit. When all is said and done, it is they who go down in defeat.

Make your plan, loved one, and check it twice---all is made ready in heaven. All awaits the leaven (change) passed on to you.

Make sure you have prayed through and find release from Me to pursue your plans. I make the adjustments as I see fit; honor Me with any final decision.

A word of caution, if you are harboring anything contrary to My will for your life, sweep the winepress clean with a full repentance. Then and only then are you clean to proceed with the mission.

I repeat, tread the winepress---make the circle complete. Tread the winepress and stay on your feet. Want to keep your balance---want to stay on top? Keep to the word and straighten out your path. Pick the flowers of praise along the way. Gather them to your bosom, then, sprinkle them before you as you go your way. Remember the leaven passed on to you. A holy calling anchored in Jesus blood. A holy calling---you keep the enemy on the run!

Get down to business---there is much to do. Get down to business---*put on both your shoes.* Obedient child of My garden---pray and love Me more. From My hands to yours, we place the grapes---just right for squeezing---until the cycle is complete

We tread the wine press together---we make the circle complete; heaven to earth---earth to heaven until we end up with processed leaven---go and conquer in My name!

ABBA   6-10-83

OVERCOMING CHINKS

Rev. 2:7

He who has an ear, let him hear what the Spirit says to the churches. To him who overcomes, I will give some of the hidden manna. I will also give him a white stone with a new name written on it, known only to him who receives it.

You have received a chink in your armor; a crack ever so small allows the enemy *inside your defenses.* There you begin to fight a losing battle.

Stop--- go no further until you repair the chink with prayer and fasting.   Fasting loosens the bond of wickedness, undoing the heavy burdens that people carry around.

Above all, be not high minded for what place has pride in your behavior? You signed on to be My disciple. I brought you to place of trusting My Word in the affairs of humankind.

When pride rears its ugly head, there and then your greatest danger comes from *within you!* Overpower these dangers with My love---for apart from Me you can do *nothing.*

ABBA   3-15-81

John 15:5

I am the vine; you are the branches. If a man remains in me and I in him, he will bear much fruit; apart from me you can do nothing.

PARTNERED WITH ME

Philip. 1:27

Only let your conversation be as it becomes the gospel of Christ: that whether I come and see you, or else be absent, I may hear of your affairs, that you stand fast in one spirit, with one mind striving together for the faith of the gospel;

You have partnered with Me in the affairs of man. You have partnered with Me in people's darkest hours. You have partnered with Me, as you shared and prayed for others.

Some were on the brink of straying; but due to your praying, they remain close to My hand.

I do not advise, nor seek to demand, that man change his divisive ways---but I will bring about swift conclusions of guidance to correct his misguided ways.

Pace yourself in the days to come. Freely drink in My word---beside the still waters. Be at peace---be at rest. Follow Me in this venture of the *saving of souls* into My hands.

Shake the dust off, as it were, from the souls of your feet, when confronted with one *who will not believe*. Turn onto My path and---walk on!

I now act on the prayers that you prayed for others. Even your name is implanted within those you have touched. Now their prayers for you will increase.

They now pour forth prayers that fill My ears on your behalf. You are blessed and loved, because you have made a difference for good in their lives.

Now My child be increased and strengthened---be increased in power to do battle for the souls of man. Follow My leading---you don't need pleading.

Return to your former ways in the daily struggle for man. Beloved---you are My child whom I love. Mete out this same love that I have for you, to man with the timing and resources given from above.

Together---we walk hand in hand as we continue our partnership in the affairs of man. I free you up to minister life and strength---as I direct.

Follow through, and build solid relationships with a word---a glance a smile---yes, be available. We walk and talk together again--- soon.

Rest now---yet in a little while I will place you in a land that needs much prayer. You can know My mind as you labor, in the spirit.

Walk on. Walk on and place your little hand into My nail scarred hand---together, man and His lord *are one!*

ABBA   2-5-91

PARTNERS—ON YOUR WAY

1 John 4:13
    We know that we live in him and he in us, because he has given us of his Spirit.

There is within the heart of *man* a desire to know his Creator. Burned deep into the soul is an agonizing drive to seek refuge in and to attach himself to the root of man's beginning.

It is that source---that spark---that unsettled drive in man that you must *tap into,* nurture, and bring forth into the light, where My Word, *the Son,* can place His healing touch, and put to rest---in the heart of man---once, for all, the *striving* of mere man to know His God and his fellow man.

O my child ---look beyond the brutish man, the timid soul, the prude, the clown, and see him as I do---naked --- stripped of all facade, all pretense, and standing truly ashamed and bewildered in the privacy of his own inner being!

Ring the chimes of grace---make haste to free mankind. Live your life for Me---O! Attached one---to My Tree, for you draw your strength from Me.

Let the fierce winds blow---Let the storms of life, bear down, as you read, praise, and pray for deliverance from the storms that come your way!

Don't frown nor fear the hand that places you here or there. We walk together---you and I. I carry you over hill and dale, even when you seem so pale, so frail, and ill at ease. I never leave My own adrift idly at sea; for I have made you well---to ride upon the crest of the turbulent waves, and help shape the world for Me!

So *partners* ---Be on your way; the vision of *ingathering of newly reborn* saints awaits your confirming nod. Shod your feet with the Gospel of love---I walk ahead of you to prepare the way!

ABBA   4-17-83

PASSING THROUGH THE VEIL

Hebrews 10:19-20

Therefore, brothers, since we have confidence to enter the Most Holy Place by the blood of Jesus, by a new and living way opened for us through the curtain, that is, his body...

There was no way to be absolved from your sins by the sacrificing of bulls and goats' blood.* (Heb. 10:4)

There was no forgiveness until I came and *paid it all* on that tree of pain and shame, once and for all times!

Now as a saved and sanctified son and daughter, you can come directly, with boldness, to the seat of My father's throne.

You have that assurance—beloveds---O! Saved and sanctified child of My heart. Ask---in faith and believing trust---anything, and I will do it---in My timing.

However--My answers are conditional, based on obedience and a lifestyle of repentance---with thanksgiving. That must always be your way of life!

Give Me your *will*, without reservation, and I will teach you more and more about kingdom living: righteousness, peace, and joy in the Holy Spirit!

Read and Re-read Hebrews 10. Soak in the Word, for it is a treasure map for kingdom living!

ABBA   9-39-08

PATHS OF SERVICE THE SAME

Psalm 25:10
   All the ways of the LORD are loving and faithful
for those who keep the demands of his covenant.

Why don't you go conquer in My name? Why not go out and receive your "flame" (Christ in you---the hope of glory)? *Flame of my youth---My hearts desire! Flame of my youth---my complete attire.*

Watch and wait---pass the gate ---the gate of human desire.

Go---conquer in My name. The place? Always the same---paths strewn about with decay----the decay of dying man. Why don't you stand against the shame---the shame of unbelief and animal desire? Some even let themselves out for hire.

Decadent man. Who can save---who can share My *plan of love*? You---you, My child, go in My name, and bring Him fame.

Stand up! We fight for man from dawn to dusk. For Jesus the king, Jesus the Lord, go out and conquer in My name. Untold hoards await your cry---untold hoards --- don't let them die!

See Him physically---a site to behold. He is heads and shoulders above the crowd; but what He sees, He passes it on to you, if you can discern His Spirit. He is like a silent Jew who observes and ponders---never speaks, and never squanders.

Pray through and rise above the crowd and see a multitude—made ready for you and for Me. Why don't you go now---go conquer in My name as you pray and cause the world to come to Him!

ABBA   6-13-83

PERFECT PEACE AND TRUST

Isaiah 26:3
   You will keep in perfect peace him whose mind
is steadfast, because he trusts in you.

Pray to Him who knows no boundaries---small or wide--- loves to challenge---often chides. Never turn away in anger when you are corrected by My hand; for those I love, I chasten as a good parent should. It builds character in the young as well as the adult!

Correction sets the boundaries of safety and character building for My beloveds and defines the freedom within those boundaries for a healthy direction and service in Me for their lives!

Royal are you, O majestic one! Yes---majestic is He who sent His son ---adorned in the robes of common man. I tell you more. You have read it in the Book---now hear it in this word.

In perfect trust He came from Me. In perfect trust He has set you free to duplicate His *feats and more!* Even nature itself agrees.

Since Jesus purchased you back through His atonement with His perfect Pascal blood shed on your behalf, returning dominion over all My creation to My children, it falls to you, and all redeemed man, to *take dominion!*

That, My son---My daughter, is your rightful heritage. Have I not recorded it in the Book ---when I declared: "Let the redeemed say so"; for I have delivered you from the grip that Satan had over you. (Ps. 107:2) By My son's obedient act, you were loosed from his foul control.

When you, of your own volition said, *"Save me Lord, and set me free from his tyrannical grip,"* you were given authority over all demonic action in the world.

Therefore, call into being that which honors Me, using the name of Jesus in your demands over the enemy. How few of My redeemed children use this authority.*   The churches at large, for the most part, only touch on this teaching, if at all.

Set them free---trusted ones.

The keys of My Kingdom turn and twist---opening doors both secret and fixed. Enlarge your boarders---the time is *now!* Reach out to encompass them who falter and say, "There is no God above." Show them and pray---until their eyes are opened and they see Me above their *torn hearts and lives. Turn them back to their King---and yours!*

ABBA

*Titus 2:11-15

For the grace of God that brings salvation has appeared to all men. It teaches us to say "No" to ungodliness and worldly passions, and to live self-controlled, upright and godly lives in this present age, while we wait for the blessed hope--the glorious appearing of our great God and Savior, Jesus Christ, who gave himself for us to redeem us from all wickedness and to purify for himself a people that are his very own, eager to do what is good. These, then, are the things you should teach. Encourage and rebuke *with all authority.*

PRACTICE YOUR HOSPITALITY

Numbers 24:5
How beautiful are your tents, O Jacob, your dwelling places, O Israel!

Practice your hospitality ministry within reason, for herein, great work is accomplished in ministering to the who-so-ever-wills---especially to those who are in great need in one form or another.

My Spirit in-fills the sanctuary of your dwelling place ten-fold during these times of committed service to bring those who-so-ever-wills to a place of understanding of what their greatest needs are as they experience the warmth of My presence in this, your dwelling place.

ABBA

PREPAREDNESS

2 Tim. 2:15
Do your best to present yourself to God as one approved, a workman who does not need to be ashamed and who correctly handles the word of truth.

148

Rush the saints to the wall---storm the gates of the troll---(demonic forces). Beggarly nymphs dare to attack My elite, My precious ones.

Rise to the fray. Contact the laggards. By prayer---bend their wills in submission to Me, using My Word.

Dawn breaks forth over the battle–ground. Survey their losses, toss them to the wind, and scatter their leaders.

Undaunted *followers of the way,* you know it pays. Never---since the *fall*---has there been such a fury of activity amongst those destined to the eternal pit.

Clean up after each contact, and present yourselves to My court. Polish the brass on your helmet---see that you stand before Me *clean.* Check your armor well. Trim the wicks and fill your lamps with oil. *Preparedness is the key.*

Fortify yourself, devour the Word, eat His body and drink His blood, O covenant keeper in the *new dimension* (New Testament). This will surely get the world's attention.

Warriors honed to a fine cutting edge; how can they stand against My beloveds? How can they stand against such might?

But still---My children, be not lulled to sleep in a false security of brilliance; for they, even now, regroup to fight, to kick and scratch---Trying to snatch you away and cause you to stray. So---*stay on the alert.* Praise, read, and pray---*we win after all!*

ABBA

RAISED TO HIGHER GROUND

Ps. 121:1-2
I lift up my eyes to the hills-- where does my help come from? My help comes from the LORD, the Maker of heaven and earth.

Is. 58:11

The LORD will guide you always; he will satisfy your needs in a sun-scorched land and will strengthen your frame. You will be like a well-watered garden, like a spring whose waters never fail.

Like a ship being guided through the 'locks' of a great canal, I have raised you step by step---to higher ground!

Like a ship sitting between rising waters within the canal, I have caused you, through your obedience, to patiently endure as My instructions and revelations come into view.

We are not through all the canals of rising water. Testing and patience have seasoned your 'keels.' Each lock entered in this controlled environment—to speak to your inner man, giving you rest and assurance for the tasks ahead, ---is guided by My strong *right hand*.

For I AM the master pilot; I know the way that I have chosen for you. I bring blessings upon you both. Continue to work in My vineyard as I, through you, bring in children and adults throughout the world, Christianizing as you walk and talk to the who-so-ever-wills, bringing them to the foot of My throne!

O! Child of the Light, this is only the beginning. You and others like you, who have turned your *wills* over to My care and keeping, serve Me with your whole heart, minds and souls.

Some have had a head start in evangelizing the world within My master plan. Never, never fear the hoards of the militant Islamic world! For in a moment of time, I will bring them to their just reward!

Continue to cry out to Me for the many now in Satan's grip to come to the *living water* and share eternity together in My family of love.

ABBA   6-12-02

REACH BEYOND THE TEMPORAL

Rev. 22:16
I, Jesus, have sent my angel to give you this testimony for the churches. I am the Root and the Offspring of David, and the bright Morning Star.

You can reach beyond the temporal and touch the "Morning Star." You can reach deep within and feel His presence! For He comes to every man even with wings studded with jade.

O! Man in modern garb---why do you press so to invade regions of the unknown, testing His hand? He will not wholly stay His hand when man, in his temptation, saunters forth in areas *not lighted* by His presence.

O! Man in ignorance---why do you ply your hand to try the doors of the world of darkness---the very darkness of carnal imaginations?

Will you never learn the lesson that *in Him is light*, and in Him, no darkness can prevail!

Come---take a drink---a deep drink of the 'waters of Life.' As you concentrate on Him, old wounds fade away. The brilliance of His flame begins to stir the wind that first brought forth that love for Him—as your heart was quickened in His presence---as you knew beyond all doubt that it was He. His hand so lovingly caring, lifted you once again into the heavenlies.

O! Reach beyond the temporal---feel the wind blow you free from wrong directions, leading you on to perfection.

For in Him is embodied the very essence of eternal life---gloriously written across that *Morning Star.*

O son---O daughter of the New Jerusalem---stretch forth your faith and trust and exercise your claim; for you are sons and daughters of the King.

Let your praise touch even the hem of His garment. Look for His coming—see Him, birthed anew, as eyes that have never seen Him suddenly see Him as He is---their Savior---Lord and King.

Reach beyond the temporal. His hand even now awaits your grasp!

ABBA   5-31-88

REBELLIOUS RESISTANCE

Proverbs 17:11
An evil man is bent only on rebellion; a merciless official will be sent against him.

Rave on, O raging one---rave on! Your flesh is determined to dominate your spirit, at times, to the point of *no return!* Why do you choose to die? Repent and turn to your God. Make a *covenant of peace* with your Maker.

Rave on, O raging one---rave on! All have sinned ---all have turned away (at times). All have used their own 'mighty' arm.

The arm withers---the heart grows faint and weary. Conniving and lawlessness appear as *fear,* and it is allowed to flourish within the flesh of men in total rebellion, oblivious to My call on their lives.

I know what man is made of, and also what man is capable of. He can rise to the heights of heaven, or sink to the deepest of pits! It is time to rise, My child, and time to receive *knowing forgiveness.*

Are you aware---have you *really* sought My face? Have you actually sought My Son? I demand that you cease from your lawlessness and *senseless fears.*

Reach out with the faith that is within you, and come home to the *nest of love, joy, peace* and an apportionment of eternal riches. They await the *repentant heart.* Your true joy and sanctuary lie in the light of the Son!

Repent! Receive My Son while you still have time. Stop your *lawlessness*---seek My face---seek My glory--- seek My joy. Frame your existence within the confines of My Word; then the Glory of the Lord your God---*will be upon you*---even in *prophetic ways!*

My love knows no bounds of forgiveness to an *obedient* and *repentant heart!*

ABBA

RENEWED TO A PLACE OF SONSHIP

Titus 3:5

> He saved us, not because of righteous things we had done, but because of his mercy. He saved us through the washing of rebirth and renewal by the Holy Spirit,

Out of the darkness of your man-made disobedience, I have called you. I have called you through My searching touch of correction. My arm is not short, as it stretches and searches the cracks and crevices---examining every inch of your *backslidden* path.

153

You are Mine, and I AM jealous over your life, for it belongs to Me. I remind you that I AM not called the, "hound of heaven" without just cause!

Eons past---it was decided to make a way possible for fallen man to be redeemed and returned to His place of sonship. I do not use fair play, as the world understands fair play, to seek and save ---to seek and restore, to protect and to build, to comfort and rebuild.

Rock upon rock---stone upon stone, cemented solidly in place with the mortar of My son's blood. No one---no one has the power to take you out of My hand.

You are a precious jewel, needed to fulfill the balance of My crown; for I have chosen this way to rule, in association with the fellowship of My children.

You are the glory of My head, and I jealously guard our relationship. *Blood bought* and precious are the saints who stand within the fold of My love and generosity—and within the power of My love.

I will reach to the very gates of hell to redeem, to pursue, to bring back into fellowship---any wayward child on the very brink a Godless eternity.

Let your hearts be quiet, and *ponder such love* that sees beyond *hopelessness,* beyond failure in the human realm, beyond *ugliness* and *filth*---once touched by the power of My gift of salvation.

Know that I see such a one---whole and complete---a child, *holy, precious* and *redeemed.* You must, as My heir, also see with My eyes ---toward any soul seeking My heart.

Live with expectation---live with excitement and anticipation. Know that you are under the cover of My Godhead, dressed in robes of brilliant white---made white by the precious *spilled blood* of the lamb.

Rest now in peace. Rest now in the knowledge that heaven itself grows brighter as each redeemed one---brought back within the fold---returns to a life of reading, hearing, and sharing My word, praising, praying and affirming the love first extended to you---through My Son---to others about you in My Name.

Love one another. Forgive one another, and encourage one another. Share Jesus with one another, and so fulfill the great commission.

Go in My name---fill the highways and by-ways. Search out the lost, the backslidden---the discouraged---those in fear and despair. Share My love. You are My hands and feet. You know My heart---now be prepared to go wherever I send you at any given moment. Reach into the darkness. Be their light to see the 'path of My returning.'

For you have the very mind of Christ!

ABBA   3-4-90

REPAIRERS OF THE BREACH

Isaiah 58:12

Our people will rebuild the ancient ruins and will raise up the age-old foundations; you will be called Repairer of Broken Walls, Restorer of Streets with Dwellings.

O repairers of the breach---gather about, and listen to My story. "There was a man---set apart for service to Me---set apart indeed. Through trial and error he stumbled on in his early youth---walking down all the *wrong paths*. A deep longing for My temple pulled and tugged at his heart. *"Boy am I smart. I can have and handle all earthly pleasures and drink deep of the nectar of life, and know and walk with my God."*

Childlike in his nature---sensitive also to Me, attacked by his own choice to *sample drugs*---he muddled on until that day I drove him into a corner---the corner of *no escape.*

"Try Me and live ---or turn away and die," I said. Face in the mud-encrusted land---without man's help---without hope.

He chose My hand upon his life---full as it was with strife, but open to the tree of his beginnings---open to the tree that allotted him extra innings.

Close to Me he came. Without shame he learned to follow Me. Then---another race appeared. His war came into full view. He went through Seminary and became a pastor of a team (changed denominations from which he was bred).

Now robed in garments of another sect and graced in another man's pulpit---with arduous commands, he brought many to My tree---brought many indeed, even though distracted by listening to *another voice,* another's *wishes.*

Listen to My plea. I remember another time, just gone by, as we gathered about to support him in his battle---"I spoke of wars being fought –using *non basic tools* of war," lies and backbiting.

Need I say more---need I ramble on? His biggest sin was the cares of this world---Trying to please a wife *in sin,* dashing My hopes for this mighty man!

Is it all lost---is it too late? By no means---go to your prayer room and pray on his behalf. Put your prayers behind his plow---*push* and *shove (in the spirit).*

He's stuck in the muck and mire of life---unable to let himself *out for hire.* Who is this wretched one? Another of My sons gone sour, trying to minister for Me as before the day he fell. But he left his back door open for the wily one---creeping in a *little at a time*, as a green smelly mold---rotting everything it touches.

Poor common man is now nothing without Me, shot down in the prime of his ministerial life.

I said, "No---go and help aid his rescue; keep in mind that the enemy works hard to destroy the Shepherd's of the sheep. Push and shove in prayer, and in love help set him free. Bind her hands, her loins, her mouth---set a guard upon this spouse. O! Yes, set her, too, free for Me---that in a certain day ahead they may renew themselves to Me."

ABBA   4-19-83

RESIST HIS DESTRUCTIVE WAYS

James 4:7
Submit yourselves, then, to God. Resist the devil, and he will flee from you.

At times the road is rough and tough to reach My path, as you have found. Face reality. Until I call a halt to his madness, Satan is still the 'god of this world.'

Become familiar with your adversary; know him well. Remember you can resist, and stop his destructive ways. Realize that you, in Christ, now cleansed and forgiven, have the capacity and duty to *curse him to the very pits of hell.* Use the authority of My name!

Never start your daily tasks without putting on your *full armor* (Eph.6: 13-17) and *praying* (Eph. 6:18). Never treat your adversary as an easy mark! He is a *formidable foe.*

I close this loving word to you this day---by reminding you that, I AM the same yesterday---today ---and always.

ABBA

REST IN THE LAND OF THE LORD

Exodus 33:14
And He said, My presence shall go with you, and
I will give you rest.

In the land of the Lord I will sojourn (temporarily)---in the
land of the Lord, I will rest. From His mighty hand I
receive His gift of love!

In total submission I allow His strong right arm to
enfold me---gently He presses me to His breast whispering,
"Rest, rest. The battle *this day* is Mine alone."

Take refuge against My chest. Who among you will let
My heart of hearts provide for your every need? In this
time of quietness, in this act of peace---know that your
angels surround you and that their hearts are at peace.

For from My heart to theirs your paths of glory are
checked and u*nderscored*; for your way was charted the
day you chose to be absorbed!

You are that vital part of My body that is equipped to
intercede, by your faith and trust in Me to answer your
prayers for them the (who-so-ever-wills)---in their darkest
hour of need!

Go now from My mountain top---go now from the court
of the Lord. Pick up your battle garments; hold your sword
high. Now stand still. The battle is Mine not yours.

Fill your hearts on My Fatherhood. Dwell upon My
son, and My very Spirit will define each warfare, letting
you know when *that battle is won!*

Take up your cross just now---hold it aloft and shout,
"Victory---victory is His. My mouth shall speak the praises
of the Lord---let all flesh bless His holy name!"

ABBA   5-1-89

158

RETURN UNDER MY PROTECTION

Isaiah 44:22
I have swept away your offenses like a cloud, your sins like the morning mist. Return to me, for I have redeemed you.

Return now, precious one, under the umbrella of My protection. Remember---stamp this word upon your heart: "I do show mercy, time and time again, but do not mistake Me for an easy mark. I also pour out justice.

When you choose to have *no covering from above*, I cannot help you. As a free moral agent you have a right to choose.

Satan is the prince of this world, and he is constantly on the lookout for those who choose to be the captain of their own ship!

Once you have chosen to follow this course of action, he will bring a tidal wave of trouble to envelope you---Yes! Even a Tsunami to the hard hearted---so fierce and devastating that you will not survive---*unless* you call on My name to save you from utter destruction.

Give Me your *will,* beloved, and I will walk you safely through this *minefield.*

Return now, precious one, under the umbrella of My protection. Remember---stamp this message upon your heart.

Keep a holy fear of me. I balance all accounts. Therefore be obedient *in all things*, and live a lifestyle of repentance!

ABBA   4-10-81

159

ROWING WITHOUT A PADDLE

Psalm 71:12
> Be not far from me, O God; come quickly, O my God, to help me.

O! God in heaven---I have bitten off more than I can chew! I heard Your call to go into all the world and make disciples for You.

In my haste to be obedient to your call, I dropped everything and started my journey. I did not stop and pray. I did not seek Your guidance and as a result wasted precious energy in futility.

I feel like I have been rowing without a paddle; the world's strong currents of opposition have left me at a loss!

I repent of not seeking Your guidance. I ask for forgiveness. Show me clearly what to do and which way to turn, and O! Lord. please chart the path ahead of me and tell me where to stop and rest.

O My son, My daughter, in your eagerness to serve Me, you are at a standstill! Lesson learned! For without My guidance, you can do nothing!

Wait on Me and I will give you rest; wisdom will follow. I AM calming the storm within your inner man; learn to do nothing in haste.

Pray much for clear direction before taking up the challenge and going in My name, to seek out those who have never received My Son.

I will free you from your troubled heart and your distress. (Ps.107:28-29) I go before you as you follow My leading. I will arrange your circumstances that will bring you victory in My name!

Remember: Your 'interruptions' are My opportunity to bring about a successful mission in all that you do. Never again leave on any journey for Me without prayer first, and praising Me; for I inhabit the praises of My children. Dear one---you walk not alone!

ABBA

SALVATION BY GRACE ALONE

Acts 15:11
No! We believe it is through the grace of our
Lord Jesus that we are saved, just as they are.

Why do you go about interpreting what I have said about salvation and grace?

I have stated through the Apostle Paul that all common man---made by My hand, should be treated as one body concerning salvation, for which My Son paid dearly---for all mankind.

Different denominations have taken upon themselves to interpret my Word to suit their core-values.

Brothers and sisters, this is an affront to Me, denying the Holy Spirit! When man chooses to follow Me, I, the Almighty One, allow the Holy Spirit---the third member of the Trinity---to reside, guide, and to direct the affairs of Man.

Unless you are willing to *plainly define the words* of My love letter---allowing My Spirit to direct you, I will spit you out of My mouth.

O can't you see how you hurt My heart of love? ---For I would have all mankind saved by grace alone and be servants for Me in the affairs of man!

Stop---I say, consider all that I have just said, and turn to Me daily---saying, "Have your own way---dear Father, have Your own way in my life. Direct my steps daily to seek out those lost, strayed, or stolen by the enemy; and them bring them back to Your throne of grace."

By faith, grace, and trust alone, I will guide you in the 'great commission' to go into all the world, and seek out down-trodden, wayward man and bring him back to his maker and redeemer!

ABBA   6-26-09

SAY A WORD TO THE INDIFFERENT ONE

Rev. 2:4
> Yet I hold this against you: You have forsaken your first love.

I say a word to your lack of interest In My word! I have something against you who are caught-up and engaged with the cares of this world. "Stop your indifferent lip service to Me!"

Come aside from the cares of this world. Soak in My word until your cares are put into *right perspective* as you put on My armor. Stand---and see me work out your circumstances.

I know your cares weigh heavily upon your heart; but search the scriptures and you will find that I have said, "Cast all your cares upon Me."

Know that the Holy Spirit, who resides in you, watches over you and is with you in all your circumstances. Trust Him now as He gives you rest and will handle all your problems one by one. Your position is to be obedient and live a lifestyle of repentance!

Then---*care worn one* ---give Me praise!

ABBA   12-10-80

SEEK EVERLASTING RELATIONSHIP

Isaiah 55:3
> Give ear and come to me; hear me, that your soul may live. I will make an everlasting covenant with you, my faithful love promised to David.

You can do this; for I know you place Me above all things that will, and are, passing away! There are natural things of beauty that I have implanted in the earth for your enjoyment.

And above all, loved ones, are the natural foods and natural medications that you can use to keep you well and strong, living a long and healthy life---in spite of what man has concocted with possible deadly side effects!

When you allow yourselves to lift your eyes up to the hills where your help comes from, (Ps. 121:1-2) you will understand!

To you who are blessed with a Christian spouse, do not go to bed until you settle your differences; you both will continue to enjoy a healthy restful sleep!

Remember *every day together is precious;* don't waste it with frivolous arguments---continue to enjoy each other in Me!

For the two of you make an unbeatable team, and all who come in contact with you will know, and see, that I AM the *central core* of your marriage!

I will bless you, with your angels protecting and guarding you both from satanic assaults. Pray and praise Me often, for "I inhabit the praises of My children."

I will answer your *believing* prayers and trust in Me for your answers. When you pray with another, they too must have the faith and trust that I *will answer* them.

163

My word is conditional on your obedience and a lifestyle of repentance! These two are the core of receiving what you ask for; I will answer your needs---not your earthly wants, when as a good father I will know what is doable or not.

Carry on until the day I bring you home to see Me face to face; then you will enjoy righteousness, peace, and joy in the Holy Spirit and be reacquainted with your family and friends that have come home before you!

ABBA   8-19-09

SEEK MY FACE O DROOPING BRANCH

John 15:2
> He cuts off every branch in me that bears no fruit, while every branch that does bear fruit he prunes so that it will be even more fruitful.

Why upon the tree are My children attached to Me? Why upon the tree are My children a delight to Me?

Because---I see them now in present form---I see them very much less than norm. But all heaven is within them now.

All in heaven and still they frown; their sins keep them from Me. Each tender branch, each stalwart limb, draws nourishment for growth from Me! I AM a jealous God who guards that which is mine---fighting for time---earth-bound children so often ashamed.

They are like that stalwart oak or redwood tree---long on endurance. O how I long to tame and direct their *limbs* so often blowing in the breeze but always staying connected to Me.

Unsettling storms buffet their leaves, leaving them limp and torn. They are constantly nourished, but seldom aware that their strength is renewed by Me. *(2 Cor. 12:9)

Their fruit I fling far from My trunk, as I fling the stars *hair-like pinions,* (wing feathers) *blown by the storm,* settling in new lands. Seeds they are---some O so small that only I---their Father, know where they lie!

But out of their struggle to survive---come forth new oaks---new redwoods to bear more limbs---more fruit, more ties to the *parent tree*; for from My breast, you must *take your rest* until I send another storm, and then off you go, over hill and dale, maturing as you go.

Seek My face, O drooping limb, and I shall make you strong; for you are committed to My care---totally belonging to Me.

See---see *I have set you free in Him!*

ABBA

2 Cor. 12:9

But he said to me, "My grace is sufficient for you, for my power is made perfect in weakness." Therefore I will boast all the more gladly about my weaknesses, so that Christ's power may rest on me.

SENSE THE MISSION WAITING AHEAD

Eph. 1:18

I pray also that the eyes of your heart may be enlightened in order that you may know the hope to which he has called you, the riches of his glorious inheritance in the saints.

Do you sense the mission waiting ahead? They are waiting for 'bread.' That bread of life is Me! O how I long to share My *body* and *blood*. O how I long for *all* to *eat* and *drink!*

You are ready to begin; I love you *selected ones*. I chose you from time in ages past. You are cut from the same mettle as Paul; he died daily for Me.

That is My impression---so get on with the lesson. Teach them the rudiments for Me; for they are not of this world---nor are you. Awake them to their potential; treat them as one as I have done. All power is given to you. (2 Tim. 1:7)

What a joy...what a thrill to praise His *skill* in recovering the lost---now *through Me*.

ABBA   6-12-80

SENSING HIS PRESENCE

Ex. 33:14
    The LORD replied, "My Presence will go with you, and I will give you rest."

I AM the Spirit of the living God, and I reside in your midst to do the work in you and My beloved people that *walk in the Way* of the Carpenter of Galilee.

You picked up your pen to write as you sensed the *nearness of My* presence. I AM all you need as you follow My plan for all to open the book and succumb to My word!

The very breath of My word testifies to the reality of eternity. For now, you have an earthly walk to learn to share---to experience the glory of the Father, Son, and My Holy Spirit.

At My call, after your work is done on this *testing ground*, we will be face to face, as you receive placement in My glorified Body.

Do you sense, My child, the nearness of My presence as expressed in the heat and tingling sensation in your hands, and know that I minister to *your* physiological needs also? O! How I love your adoration of Me, My children. O! How I love your faith and trust in Me! O! How I love the assurance as you ask in faith for the healing works of My hands through you, dear son and daughter of obedience!

Yes, I heal you in part, little by little. Yes, I heal you in total---areas of your bodily temple. Yes, I use you among believers and unbelievers alike.

You are a willing testimony to all the who-so-ever-wills, bringing them to the foot of My throne for redemption and eternal life.

Yes! I use you, as I *will* to the glory and salvation of souls that I long to bring into My kingdom.

Never question the plans I have for you! As the word says, I use you "for good and not for evil—to give you a future and a hope." (Jer. 29:11-12)

Be a light upon a hill for all to see and come to your *watering hole* (home) to drink their fill of My goodness. I heal you for all eternity. Rest and trust Me now blessed children of Mine---I love you so!

ABBA   10-30-06

SHEPHERD TO THE SHEEP

Isaiah 55:4
    See, I have made him a witness to the peoples, a leader and commander of the peoples.

Look to the Lord of Life and pay heed to My word! Prepare to sit under instruction as I, through the word, prepare you for delving into the minds and manners of these, My children. They are babes, not quite ready to understand salvation and teaching, or to *graze* in the fields of understanding.

Help them to *unlock* the gates of their *captivity*. Pull forth from their loins their emotions never before dealt with.

You are a part of a *core* that I AM calling to restore their health, direction, and *freedom in spirit*. Build your *own strengths* as I place you, along with others of *like stature*, to open their minds, hearts, and souls to receive hallowed instruction as they sit before *your seat of teaching!*

Let your spirit *spring forth* as you take your place of leadership. And now, beloved, shepherd the sheep that will be given into your charge!

ABBA   6-22-87

Note to the reader: This was the first word of my wife Jean's "Commission Call" to all the who-so-ever-wills who crossed her path!

SHOW ME YOUR WAY

Acts 16:17

This girl followed Paul and the rest of us, shouting, "These men are servants of the Most High God, who are telling you the way to be saved."

O to know you more deeply, I praise You for placement in your tree—For you have, by Your written word through your servants shown me the way! Glory to God, the gap between us draws closer; forgive me Lord if I seem anxious!

Don't fret, don't stew—I am working through you!

Through me O Lord---Through me you say?

Yes, My child; so be full of joy. Take your stand and see the babes in Christ that you nourish, attaching them to My tree.

Nurture them in the word---follow up in their progress to know Me in the deeper things that I have placed within the pages of My love letters. (Bible)

Tell them about finding that pearl of great price (Jesus), and never tire of well doing; remember ---they are new babes in kingdom living.

And, when they fall off the path along the way, remind them that all My promises are true, but conditional, based on their obedience, and a lifestyle of repentance

Find Me more---find them for Me, beloved.

ABBA   3-16-80

SIGN POSTS

Exodus 33:14
The LORD replied, "My Presence will go with you, and I will give you rest."

Quiet yourselves, and rest in Me!

You hurry through life, missing all 'signpost' messages from Me:

In Nature . . .

In Circumstances . . .

Yes---even within your own spirit---as I speak a word of encouragement to your *bone-weary* lives.

Fear not, little one, fear not---Learn to trust Me more. When the storms of life weigh you down, call on Me, and I will quiet the turbulent waters that threaten to engulf you

ABBA

Jer. 33:3
Call to me and I will answer you and tell you great and unsearchable things you do not know.'

SIN IS SETTLED

Hebrews 10:17
Then he adds: "Their sins and lawless acts I will remember no more."

Our love for you spilled over and demanded clarity for all of My created beings. That is why the law was originally given to My children; but it was only a shadow of good things to come. (Heb. 10:1)

Since then My Son, once and for all, settled all sin that so easily besets My children.

Jesus' sacrifice put the condemnation of sin to rest and by His death on the cross broke sin's domination over My children.

Since I gave man the right to choose *life* or *death, man can now be freed from hell's grip.* I provided a door of salvation for My beloved children.

My heart remains heavy, for so many have chosen to keep one foot in the world for all of its acclamations, and the other foot awaiting heaven's reward.

My child---this cannot be! Either I have all of your love and godly attention---or---you can enjoy the *fleeting* accolades of the world!

I do not say that you cannot enjoy satisfaction from your work or play; but I caution you---don't place them over Me; for I AM a jealous God and will have no other gods before Me! (Josh 24:15).

ABBA   9-11-09

SING A SONG OF WORSHIP

Psalm 98:1
Sing to the LORD a new song, for he has done marvelous things; his right hand and his holy arm have worked salvation for him.

To those who are My children in the spirit, I say, "Sing a song of worship...sing a song of praise!"

Lift your hands to the glory of the Father.   Lift your hands to the Spirit, and the Son. Rejoice in Me as one who has, in the spirit, touched the hem of My garment; for I would that all would be healed in body, soul, and spirit! Watch and pray. See My mighty right arm of heavenly justice prevail where man's earthly justice *cannot*!

I---I AM the Lord...The God of your fathers.   Be strengthened in the knowledge that you are welded to My very Being.

This earth is but a testing ground; purifying events are allowed to come your way as I strengthen you along the *way* toward your heavenly home . . .and Mine!

ABBA

SKIN DEEP

Ps. 55:17
Evening, morning and noon I cry out in distress,
and he hears my voice.

You are skin deep on everything in life, especially in prayer and praise to Me! There are times when you come to the realization that you are actually talking to Me---the Father, Son and Holy Spirit!

During those times---when you know in your heart of hearts, at the Spirit's prompting, that you really have broken through your doubts and unbelief, leaving your flesh behind--- then you are totally opened to speak to My Spirit in your quiet time of rest, leaving the world and all its frustrations behind you.

These are those precious moments when we, together, commune as one!

ABBA

SOAK IN THE WORD

Psalm 119:105
Your word *is* a lamp to my feet and a light for my
path.

Do not neglect My Word. Make it your guiding light. For where My saving light illumines the way, you can see the twists, the turns, the pitfalls, put there by his evil hand to deter you from the course that is *always* set before you.

Tell others. Show them by example that I do not leave them rudderless. I always steer My beloveds to a safe and sure harbor.

Remember, I AM your safe haven. I died and rose again to begin the chain of eternal life regardless of strife!

Keep your eyes on My 'homing beacon' (the word) and safe eternal harbor. Know you are loved. Never cease bringing others to Me in prayer---your highest call!

ABBA

SOUND JUDGEMENT ASSURES VICTORY

I Cor. 6:2
Do you not know that the saints will judge the world? And if you are to judge the world, are you not competent to judge the trivial cases?

Before you lies ahead intensive study of My word. I will give you clarity of thought, and at times a *Rhema* word--- *one that stands out to you as you read it*---that opens doors into the ministry of the Godhead. (Jesus is the Word, God's speech uttered from God's mind.) (John 1:1)

This takes dedication and perseverance. In essence you must be sold out to Me and the tasks that I set before you, with total obedience to My beck and call. I will show you hidden things---fenced in things that you do not know.

Share them with family and friends alike, that they too may grasp the *call* on their lives. What matters when I call you to listen to My heartbeat for common man?

You, My son, my daughter, are enlisted in the army of the Master of the universe. When your heart is stirred by My presence---in the daytime or the wee hours of the night---be attentive to My voice speaking to your inner man.

We have work to do, loved one, in this lawless nation, to honor and protect our fellow man, especially the elderly, who at this very moment are considered by your present administration as useless to your society.

The current leaders of this government are not making sound judgments---but are being motivated by the god of this world, trying to rid themselves of the elderly and the incapacitated. To assure victory for the righteous, "Choose you this day whom you will serve." (Josh. 24:15)

Come to Me all you who labor and are fearful, and I will give you rest and protection.

ABBA   8-21-09

SOWN A PERISHABLE BODY

1 Cor. 15:42
    So will it be with the resurrection of the dead. The body that is sown is perishable, it is raised imperishable....

Adam set the pattern in the Garden, and sinned against his Maker. His wife, Eve, when she gave him an apple and said, "Take and eat..." of this (forbidden fruit), set the stage for all humanity to *miss the mark* of a loving father!

Adam's sin doomed all of mankind to labor for his living, and he was dismissed from the *Garden of plenty* to toil and clothe himself, and his wife, by taking an animal's life to do it, spending the rest of his short life here on earth, laboring for sustenance.

But God---in his love for man---sought to bring him back into the fold. It grieved My heart to do this but I will not, cannot tolerate *disobedience* in *any form!*

I gave man a *free will* to choose---but Satan, the prince of this world, entered the scene and took man where he did not want to go!

So I sent My Son to pay the *awesome price* for sin, once and for all times. He settled the score; for Satan could not, and would not, change Jesus' allegiance to Me!

Christ, who became *true man*, brought created man, once again, into harmony with His God, and yours, beloved!

You who have chosen to follow Him and *His ways*, laboring in the fields of mankind in service to Me---by giving over your *wills* to Me, gave me the freedom to constantly direct your paths to bringing the who-so-ever wills to My throne of grace.

Until that day, when your work is done and you will be like a seed that is planted and grown to its full potential and has then fallen back onto the ground.

A *perishable man*, now raised an imperishable body to live forever---in My kingdom along with those loved ones who have gone on before.

Enjoying all of eternity with loved ones forever!

ABBA

SPEAK TO THE DARKNESS

Acts 26:16

Now get up and stand on your feet. I have appeared to you to appoint you as a servant and as a witness of what you have seen of me and what I will show you.

Speak to the darkness --speak out I say, and don't delay. Stretch forth your *withered hand* and say, "Be gone; darkness has no part of me." And so I command you to flee and test your roots in yet another place---a place of *sinking sand.*

Take your hands off My beloveds for they are covered with a cloak of love! The very winds about you are blown from My lips of love.

Venture forth---step, by step without regrets, and you will soon see the *way made straight* and clearly marked---"This is the way---walk you in it."

Do not stray. What price, what price ---you say? Your life O son O daughter---lay it down today! Jesus is all you need; for out of Him flows rivers of *life giving water.*

Thirst after righteousness---thirst after Me. I make you to become part of Me! I make you into a son, a daughter---fitted and groomed for palatial living.

Just for now---practice to acquire palatial giving. Give like a king---tried and true.

What giving, O Lord, do you require?

Give up your life to Me, and I will dole you out and mold you as potter's clay---to fulfill My needs right here on earth... in a land, sick and dying---a land full of hurts.

Yes, I will dole you out in many ways---here and there, as I choose. Until your mission is complete, and I cause your feet to stand on yet another promised land---your true eternal home.

Your *call* is high---your *call* is holy; for your *call* is from Me!

ABBA   2-20-83

STAND AND BE MY WITNESS

1 Cor. 16:13

Be on your guard; stand firm in the faith; be men of courage; be strong.

Dear child, blessed by God, whose path has trod over rugged terrain, you have reaped were others have sown. You have longed to see My face in all that you do.

O dear one, you have passed the test by leaning on Jesus, and have come to a place of rest!

The rest you seek is *never free*, for He paid the price dearly---upon the tree. Troubles drag you down? Give them over to Me, and do not frown. *I make all things new, My little lamb.*

From your hands and heart already spent---sharing the love of Jesus---entering tent after tent (homes), develop your ministry of *reckless love*, for you dare to worship without fear of risking rejection!

Launch out into the deep. Concentrate on Me. Rough and rugged paths, shunned by some, are never a problem when, with My Son---you *take His hand!*

Now---locked arm in arm you can, and will, take a stand for Him---who conquered and paid it all! Nothing too large---or too small, for Him.

Continue to be My witness. (Acts 8:35) Don't marvel at *small group ministry*, and My Spirit's penetration. Yours is a *pick-up* ministry of *great importance,* one on one. A message here---a message there.

Be steady, be faithful---always be ready. Keep it up. Listen for My voice and –keep going---beloved.

Be fruitful and multiply. Never be shy, for in so doing, My kingdom continues to grow!

ABBA   11-28-1998

Acts 8:35

Then Philip began with that very passage of Scripture and told him the good news about Jesus.

STAND FAST IN THE LORD

Phil. 4:1

Therefore, my brothers, you whom I love and long for, my joy and crown, that is how you should stand firm in the Lord, dear friends!

There is a time---night or day---deep in the recesses of His eternal Spirit, where a time of man's vulnerability is God's opportunity to reach out *un-restrained* and touch man's eternal spirit!

Deep in the recesses of man, through adversity or physical suffering, the door to the inner man is *set ajar* at the precise moment that the light and love of the Father--- through His son and comforting Holy Spirit---*burst forth* into and through that door---beckoning man's eternal spirit to come forth in communion with the Lord of the universe!

All spiritual senses *now enhanced* by that power of the Holy Spirit, he takes a full measure of unrestrained love--- unconditionally.

Man is ushered into the *Holy of Holies*; there, in love, the intent and understanding of God's *written and projected Word* blossoms into *true reality!*

Here, in this setting---the Father is able to *cut through* all the earthly restraints bound up in mortal clay, shattering that clay mold that man inhabits!

At these moments, where man's mortality is *sharply defined,* God the Father reaches down and into that place of the inner man---energizing and sensitizing his eternal spirit.

Make a choice, O Man. Make a choice: serve Me and live, or step aside and *die.*

For I still look for those who will *stand in the gap*--- awaiting instruction and *purpose* for their life. Will you *rise to the challenge?* Will you willingly follow My plan? I have much work ahead for that man---that woman who

keeps their *door ajar* ---that I may come in and out with
impunity *(no restraints)*.

ABBA   12-1-91

John 12:36
   Put your trust in the light while you have it, so that you
may become sons of light." When he had finished speaking,
Jesus left and hid himself from them.

STAND IN THE CENTER OF MY WILL

John 7:17
   If anyone chooses to do God's will, he will find
out whether my teaching comes from God or
whether I speak on my own.

Stand fast---and shake the dust of that bad-mouthed person
whose aim was and is to *steal your peace.*   But I have
silenced his mouth. Pray for that tormented one whose soul
was stolen for Satan's use.
   Think it not strange when the attacks come your way.
Stay in the center of My *will*---We fight from that
placement point. The advantage is ours and so We, in
victory---in this very hour, devour and conquer for Christ.
   Carry on, dear child,---just beware, during periods of
calm. Strengthen and *lash down* loose supports (areas of
weakness) during times of stress when gale force winds
come your way.
   Stand and watch Me work on your behalf!
   We are in a race for the souls of man, and as many as
can be, through you, beloved, must be brought into My
fold. Use your God-given gifts, with much prayer and
fasting to do so!

179

I know that you are up to the task---bringing them in ---
to Me!

ABBA

STAND MIDST THE STORM AND STRIFE

Eph. 6:13
Therefore put on the full armor of God, so that
when the day of evil comes, you may be able to
stand your ground, and after you have done
everything, to stand.

The ravages of warfare tear unmercifully into the soil of
God's beloveds. The ravages of war twist---turn, uproot,
and shake the very foundations of the faithful.

Evil rides the very winds blown out from the depths of
hell. Like an open sore straining for signs of healing, My
children are seeking rest---but none is available, for we are-
--at war!

Vicious servants pour forth into the very breach of the
weapons of My warriors. Be not overcome, for I have
begun a work that shall not fail---and shall not be
overcome!

Run to the storehouse---stand by your ambushments.
Load and *lock the powder in place.* Light the fuse and press
the trigger. Rock their brood back upon their *black-hearted*
beings.

As children of the King, use My authority. Send them
to the pit! He rose to clear the way. He rose and is with
you even now to support and steady your hand. Fear not,
beloveds, those that stand *midst the storm and strife.*

The hurricane winds of evil are upon you. You shall prevail; for I AM great and mighty to perform all that I have promised! Brace your backs against the onslaughts.

O see Me now with your inner eyes. It is I ---it is Me--- *we work and fight together*. Never look back. I say, "Never look back!" Stand tall as I know you can---in quiet strength. (2 Cor.12: 9) Concentrate on Me. Satan longs to leave My children---bloody, torn, and defeated.

He laughs with glee, just to disturb, and sack the land. But glory to My name---I put energy to good use; for in his fury he has tilled (*awakened*) the soil of My children's spirits and broken up the fallowed ground.

Are you confused, torn, and bloody? I remind you that only victory songs spring forth from the heavenly hosts. Beloved---you are free---free now to plant---to rake through wind-swept land. Free to realign and reshape the paths.

Smell honeysuckle---* it is just the perfumed breath of your angels passing across your nostrils, as you labor together with others of like mind. Your angels surround your tent with their praises to Me on your behalf.

Dear heart---you stand not alone!

ABBA

Eph. 6:14
Stand firm then, with the belt of truth buckled around your waist, with the breastplate of righteousness in place.

* Dear Reader,
In the last two years of her life, my wife was attended by 'her angel,' whom she called Rose because of the aroma that filled the air. Jean would say, "Rose is here; I can smell her aroma!"

*One day in the last few months of her life she said,
"Rose, your aroma has changed." Rose said to Jean (in the
spirit), "It is not my aroma you smell ---it is the Father's
aroma!"*

*Now a rose, with the stem and leaves, has been etched
on the flat black granite head stone, next to Jean's name.*

STAY AWAY FROM LOVING MONEY

Hebrews 13:5

Keep your lives free from the love of money and
be content with what you have, because God has
said, "Never will I leave you; never will I forsake
you."

Beloved---that the love of money is the root of all evil is
true, and Satan waves the money flag before all of
mankind!

This is the petrol (gasoline) that is taught to your youth
in their formative years, and the uninformed of all of your
society.

Driven and touted over the airways and television
commercials, and believed by greed, is the way to quick
riches.

Money of itself is *not evil*---it is the love of it that
consumes your waking hours. You are bombarded by the
powers that be---to make all you can, one way or another.

My children---this ought not to be. As a tool to buy the
items necessary to your life, *yes!* As an instrument in
tithing, *yes!* To help a fellow in need, *yes!*

All these things are avenues of being a good steward.
Don't let Satan beguile (mislead) you into thinking that the
prime reason for your finances is to glorify self, and satisfy
all your fleshly desires!

It is also used, in moderation, for enjoyment in the pursuit of your needs, not *your wants!*

Put in right prospective, it can, and does, provide for much needed vacations and moderate pleasures.

Don't get caught-up in the abuse of money; this world is not your home, beloveds. Stay on the alert. Staying in balance will provide you with all you need to serve Me and common man.

When you see a brother or sister in need, *"Give, and it will be given to you. A good measure, pressed down, shaken together and running over, will be poured into your lap. For with the measure you use, it will be measured to you." (Luke 6:38)*

Do this, loved one, in service to your fellow man, and also to Me!

ABBA   7-24-09

STAY FOCUSED

Is. 30.21

Whether you turn to the right or to the left, your ears will hear a voice behind you, saying, "This is the way; walk in it."

Stay focused. Guard the sheep. Record the events that led you to My feet; for at the cross, I paid it all, for man, woman and child.

Parch the earth, son of this universe. Man in his greed upset the order of nature's way; I use you for good, and for punishment.

My gifts, always meant for good, include a two-edged sword lying in wait to punish at My command; stay My hand of wrath—you who watch for Me.

Come, kneel and pray with Me; for I still long for you to pray at My side. I still long to feel the warmth of your body next to Mine (position) as we wrestle for common man—underneath a King---waiting for the former and latter rain to set him free, standing tall in a new heaven and a new earth, when all will be made right!

We march with the "church triumphant." Sweet songs of pleasant smelling jasmine, cover the universe in an umbrella of love!

Cry victory My sweet. Cry victory indeed. Glory to the Father—glory to the Son—glory to the Spirit, blessed three in one!

ABBA   1-17-99

STAY ON THE COURSE

Genesis 12:3
I will bless those who bless you, and whoever curses you I will curse; and all peoples on earth will be blessed through you."

Stay on the course of study that you have undertaken and will continue to undertake.

I'm going to show you things that you can hardly imagine, not only for your good---but also to further the ministry of helping others walk in the way of the cross.

Bless others as I continue to bless you. I love you deeply, sincerely, forever, and ever . . .O! child of My heart.

Be blessed!

ABBA

Genesis 22:18
...and through your offspring all nations on earth will be blessed, because you have obeyed me.

STRETCH FORTH YOUR HAND

Matthew 12:13
Then he said to the man, "Stretch out your hand." So he stretched it out and it was completely restored, just as sound as the other.

Stretch forth your hand in faith, and be established in the truth. Whatever I give your hands to do---do it as unto Me.

Willing hands, willing feet, willing spirit all framed within the body of believing children thwarts the enemy and brings about his defeat.

You live and work in rapidly changing times. Work while it is yet day---'soon comes the night when no man can work.'

Live in an attitude of prayer---expect the unexpected. Do you sense the shaking by My hand (earthquakes)?

Count the cost of discipleship; and if after you have counted the cost, you still desire to walk on in *My footsteps, do not look back.* Once you put your hand to 'the plow' walk on---making a firm straight furrow.

Plant the seeds of life---cover them with loam (rich soil), water them with the Word. Once you commit your life to the plowing, the seeding and the watering, *do not look back.* Walk on with hands, heart, and feet in the spirit of faith---I say, "Walk on and continue to cultivate the sheep."

Watch therefore, and pray. The Spirit and the Word say, "Come---encircle one another with prayer."---Come now toss your gauntlet into the fray---while it is day, for I am coming again in an hour yet unannounced. Watch therefore. Keep to the book. Read, praise, and pray---for we are in agreement, dear child; continue to pray for the lost, the lonely, and the weary---tarry 'till I come---I *will come quickly.*

I take you by the hand just now and touch it to My breast. Be at rest---be at peace you are loved---more than you can comprehend.

It is enough to know that you are loved---be established in My truth---it will *set you free!*

ABBA   12-8-89

STRIVE TO ENTER INTO MY REST

Hebrews 4:11
    Let us, therefore, make every effort to enter that rest, so that no one will fall by following their example of disobedience.

Do you see how that angel of light has so greatly fallen, he who wanted to be God over Me? Your finite mind cannot comprehend the depths that he has fallen to, and the danger to My beloveds.

I have done and continue to do great battles through My angels on all your behalf. Strive to the letting of blood, if need be, to continue on and in My light, loving the brethren---upholding and interceding for: brother, sister, husband, wife and children—and the communion of the saints!

Strive to enter into My rest. Put past and present sins behind you ---in true repentance and walk on.

As you read, praise, and pray---rise above this world's, and your own, madness. Learn the wiles of him and be sensitive to his devices.

Be careful to note his seductive manners. He would, and does, strive to disarm even My very elect! I am outraged that he dares to harm the 'apple of My eye.' (Ps. 17:6)

A defeated foe is he. You must stay on the alert---in this your continuing trial----to be that man or woman of the hour, My minute-men, and women.

They, when armed by My Spirit---can calm the seas, dispel the fiery darts---walk over the flaming coals laid down by his hand and *untimely* reach, trying to keep you from your haven of rest.

Now then---brush yourself clean with the Word. Pickup your protective armor, and place it about you. Now pick-up the 'sword of the spirit;' be strong in the strength of My Spirit.

Stand against the schemes of the devil; for your struggle is not against flesh and blood, but against the ruler of this present world. Remember you do the standing, and I do the fighting.

Now remove your armor, and escort all the who-so-ever-wills--- that will enter into the banquet feast--and eternal rest!

ABBA   4-26-89

SUBMISSION THROUGH FORGIVENESS

Eph . 1:7
In him we have redemption through his blood, the forgiveness of sins, in accordance with the riches of God's grace...

187

Reach out to your God, and say, "Forgive me." Reach out to your God and pray. Noteworthy prayers filter into His light. Noteworthy prayers always His delight..

Don't struggle; don't stew---reach out in love, and capture the Jew---the Gentile---unbelievers all. Reach out in love; don't let them fall!

What can I do---I cannot see---What can I do but believe? Reach down deep and spare their lives.

My child---Concentrate on living, and love your fellow man. Seek out Jesus as He gives His direction in love.

Weigh the balance of the scale---stay the hand that can say, "you have been weighed in the balance and found wanting." (Job. 31: 6)

O Stretch forth your hand and see it gather strength---O stretch forth your hand is My command. Send forth a force of love; for as you pray and praise Me more---directing your prayers of love--your prayers gather wings, and your faith is sent forth. Do it all for Me; for from My hands to you, I give the vitality of Spring.

O reach out to Me just now, and say, "Forgive, O tender and loving Father." I long to gather My children to Me. Satan's wrath is *divided* each time you *transmit* your love to Me, and to the who-so-ever-wills that cross your path. Teach them about My son, bring them up in the faith, then---ask them to commit themselves to Him!

ABBA   5-31-83

TAKE HEART

Job 4:6-7

Should not your piety be your confidence and your blameless ways your hope? "Consider now:

Who, being innocent, has ever perished? Where were the upright ever destroyed?

Take heart . . .I am working out the plans for your life, day-by-day. Fear not; My Spirit goes before you, clearing the path for your daily progress in Me!

Make *more time* in the study of the Word, especially in the early evening hours to strengthen your faith and trust through committed prayer--- and, for the faith and trust in others as you cross their paths and they seek council from you.

Continue to be that *light* and *hope*---for others to see the *steadfast, unmovable* witness you exhibit, as they receive comfort and relief from the path of their travail!

ABBA

Job 13:15
Though he slay me, yet will I hope in him; I will surely defend my ways to his face.

Job 11:18
You will be secure, because there is hope; you will look about you and take your rest in safety.

TAKE YOUR HEALING WITHOUT COST

2 Samuel 24:24
But the king replied to Araunah, "No, I insist on paying you for it. I will not sacrifice to the LORD my God burnt offerings that cost me nothing." So David bought the threshing floor and the oxen and paid fifty shekels of silver for them.

189

Take your healing without form or price. There is much work to be done. Come now; take your release in Me.

Now get on with the tasks that I have set before you; this day---this very hour---with the power given you from above, cross over into the land of decision and belief.

What a relief. What joy. What indescribable love! For He, my King, has set me free, and now I walk in His love bringing all whom I touch into the valley of decision, established by His love!

ABBA   3-5-80

TASTE THE WATER JUST NOW

Psalm 34:8
   Taste and see that the LORD is good; blessed is the man who takes refuge in him.

I trouble the waters that man may be healed---I trouble the waters until---in that *'God-awakened hour'*---My life is revealed.

O taste the water just now---taste and see that it is good. Taste and see that I understand how fragile man is!

Take just now. See, I have given My blood to set you free. Yes—washed by the blood of the Lamb. He became true man for you. Nailed to the tree, He was held in check; held by sin, and sent to death on the cross for you.

Son of the dust—You are free---for He could not be held by the power of hell. For man He arose. So follow Him where He leads. Follow 'We Three'-- Never forget that as you walk the paths he trod . . . you never walk alone!

For I AM always with you!

ABBA   11-14-80

TEMPORARY PAIN

Job 33:19
Or a man may be chastened on a bed of pain
with constant distress in his bones...

Light the torch---now grasp it in your hand in the dark shadows of your life. No time for complacency. Though pain and discomfort overshadow you---hold high the torch of liberty, for I have set you free.

Reckon that the pain and suffering in this worldly shell is only temporary. I allow it to deepen your dependency on Me.

Who or what is man that they may mock you? O! I have set you free to roar and soar. Be a delight to Me in this hour of strengthening.

Champion of My trust---O warrior, at My command. Rise above the purifying pain and discomfort. Discover again---My place of rest.

Yes, this is only a test; ---remember, loved one, stay in the *nest* until the trumpet sounds, and you realize the quest. The quest is ---that you, My beloved, were made for Me---- for My joy and satisfaction.

When you have been released from the pain---physical or mental---carry on with the full knowledge that I continue the perfection in you for greater and still---*greater work!*

Labor only to enter into My rest. You and yours be encouraged as you lift high the torch. Be that light in whatever part of this world I place you in.

Reach into all the dark corners of this world, in prayer through that lighted torch---which ---My beloved ---*is Me!*

Darkness always gets our attention. Remember: "You will learn the most about My principles and faithfulness in the *dark seasons* of your life!"

191

During these times---listen and do not question My sovereignty. Always walk toward the light of a *new day*. Remember: "What you learn in the darkness---share with others in the light and glory of My Son."

ABBA

THAT PEARL OF GREAT PRICE

Matthew 13:46
Again, the kingdom of heaven is like a merchant looking for fine pearls. When he found one of great value, he went away and sold everything he had and bought it.

Hidden among the stones is that "pearl of great price!" Hidden among the stones is a heart that weeps---a heart that seeks the lost and confined.

For every man, woman, and child---bears within his breast that spirit, that counterpart of God which longs to be set free and mate with its *life giving half*.

For we are not yet one---we are not whole, until that breath of His Spirit rests within our inner man.

Who can know the depth of deception---a solid mass caked over our spirit. It has been layered-over there, by man himself, apart from his God; but as we are touched by His very breath, we immediately look for, and long for, that "pearl of great price" from among the stones.

For Jesus still walks among the stone*s*---the *stones of life* to this very day---through you. Searching, ever searching for His *counter part* that will turn to its maker and declare, "I have been bought with a price"--- that no earthly money can match.

I have been bought with a price, and I need no longer scratch among the rubble to find that pearl; for from it radiates the breath of life, and I can feel all of eternity beckoning me to follow, to be absorbed, to live my life in His grasp; and for His sake. Now at last---I am free to soar.

To follow the shorelines of the world for man without his God, in Christ, is but another stone impaled, and lost, in the *sands of time.*

Stand up---follow Him, wherever He leads; for He is taking you home, to Kingdom living of righteousness, peace, and joy (rejoicing) in the Holy Spirit!

ABBA   11-2-88

THE BATTLE RAGES ON

Romans 7:23
...but I see another law at work in the members of my body, waging war against the law of my mind and making me a prisoner of the law of sin at work within my members.

The main battle lies ahead in the inner man---where stripped of his costume for all to see---he, the tempter himself, plunders and snatches many from Me.

Stand tall---eyes forward ---locked arm in arm. We are coming in prayer and deed. O, suffering ones, we are coming as one into the fray---recovering the lost and all who will say, "You have opened God's words to us and made it plain. We know you care as you share your love. Our hearts cry out---you are a friend indeed!

Their eyes do not see, as do you. ---They only see Me in the form of God's people holding out their hands in words of love.

193

Dear children of My heart, the battle rages on, fighting for the lost and confused---those shaken by the events of the day. Keep praying---keep reading the Word.

Let praise to Me be your song. I'm moving you through the mine–fields that are surrounded by legions of angels. Fret not---you are not alone!

Nothing will harm you as you walk upon the water of: *trusting faith in Me!* Believing faith and patience---is the truth that keeps you free in Me.* (Heb. 6:12)

When your allotted time on earth has passed, you will enter My gates, at last to *rest* from the raging battle. Then I will gather you to My breast---there to enjoy the fruits of your inheritance, gathering with the other saints --- worshipping and glorifying Me, as we *busy ourselves* together throughout eternity!

For now--- courage---stay the course, secure in your armor.* (Eph. 6:13) Now raise My banner of victory high and---*stand!*

ABBA

*Hebrews 6:12

We do not want you to become lazy, but to imitate those who through faith and patience inherit what has been promised.

*Eph. 6:13

Therefore put on the full armor of God, so that when the day of evil comes, you may be able to stand your ground, and after you have done everything, to stand.

THE BONDAGE OF SIN BROKEN

Romans 8:21

...that the creation itself will be liberated from its bondage to decay and brought into the glorious freedom of the children of God.

Take your pen in hand, O child of Mine and say to My beloveds, those that took that step of faith---that step that put them in right relationship with Me: "I see you standing there perplexed and broken. I see you standing in ashes and smoldering. Life's ambitions crushed? Wild fantastic dreams nonplused (embarrassed)---melted away by every whim of man?"

Man in a fallen state, monitored by another. Who is this one; surely not My son? But the evil one comes to distort---disclaim, tear down, and kill. He is the unholy one---on the dark side of the hill---he, he *is the one!*

Cry out to Him who paid it all---cry out to Him even as did St. Paul. Blinded by the light? Or eyes tightly shut lest the light of Him who conquered all *reveal your sin?* Come in, come in to *sup* and dine with Him, and have fellowship with the Father.

You people live like *swine most of the time*, groveling in the mud; when all the time, I take My stand---just a shade removed from your hand.

I stand there, firmly fixed, at the edge of the pit---holding out to you your royal garments---to you who are in despair.

Why do you lie there in hopelessness and ruin?

Why do you lie there forlorn and depressed? Look about you---all you see is, *plaster ---and disaster;* but it came not from Me!

Awake---awake mischievous one. Awake. Awake. Stand up. Rise out of the slum---the slum of the earthbound *sense-type living*; the slum of your hardness of heart in *unforgiving that one---so close to you---so near, ---the one you should be out to cheer and encourage,* as I have done---*for you.*

ABBA

THE CHAIR OF AGREEMENT

Psalm 113:4
The LORD is exalted over all the nations, his glory above the heavens.

In the land that time forgot---great issues have their sway.
In the land that time forgot---all layers are peeled away!
Gone is the pretence---the sham---the pride. Each layer that is peeled away—reveals more of the Savior's heart. His person fills the expansion of the ever-increasing universe.

Galaxies, yet undiscovered by man, know the heart of His hand. His Word unbounded ricochets across each land. Each timeless expanse of space---we are overcome by the bigness (expansion) of His Spirit which knows no bounds!

His Glory, radiant and pure, shines forth in brilliance as freshly driven snow, into that realm, beloveds, ---into that realm where your prayer and praises enter in.

The prayers, expectations and fulfillments, soar free with answers found! For in that land of time forgotten--- the law of intercession has its root!

The simplest or gravest petition when offered in Jesus' name---resounds like anthems of greatest stature, free from earthly strain. O child of God, learn the meaning of prayer.

Collectively we enter My chamber of reasoning---come quickly---I offer you a chair---it is a *chair of agreement,* a chair where our spirits meet.

It is the chair of agreement---borne aloft with by angels' feet, swift to comply with our judgment---swift to bring to naught Satan, with his limited power.

No task too small...no task too large can stand against us in the fight for common man, and for the land---for freedom to conquer. No man or dark angel, no discord of any kind, can stand between us in our relationship in the endless expanse of timelessness!

So very few answer the call. Set aside your shackles. Set aside your fear of pain. Gain not the world and all its passions. "Seek Me and you shall find."

For to know Me is pure wisdom in the land that time forgot.

Come now in worship. The reign is ours. Come---I have prepared your crown ---your very robes lie at My feet in readiness for your *glorified form*. Until that day of final departure and inaugural ball, feel free to enter--- ever so often. My love awaits your *daily arrival* (in the spirit).

Stand tall against the fall!

ABBA   5-6-89

THE DANGER OF UNFORGIVENESS

Mark 11:25
And when you stand praying, if you hold anything against anyone, forgive him, so that your Father in heaven may forgive you your sins.

Your life is released to the person that you forgive! You *free* people made in My image as you release them. Unforgiveness is *binding*.

You literally strap a person down---when you do don't---or won't forgive them!

You may tend to pin people down to what they are not---or have not yet become--- when you think that they should be in a more mature state!

Dear child---be *patient* with *persistence* to follow through with forgiveness. They are growing in the faith; but maybe not as fast as you would like them to be.

Therefore you tend to block and restrict their growth in Me by your *unforgiving spirit*---verbally or non verbally!

Loved one, as exceptional as *long suffering* is, it is not a license to disobey Me or to become *puffed up* by reading My word every day without forgiving your fellow man's digressions. *Repent quickly!*

Begin the liberation process of bringing them, in love, by forgiving their *unforgiveness*; or---if they don't accept your act of forgiveness, release them to the enemy so he can *work his way with them!*

This is not a vindictive act on your part---as you remove your protective prayers from them; hopefully it will lead them to repentance!

It is impossible to go through life and not be discouraged at times. During those hard days---act like David of old---when he cried out, "Search me, O God, and know my heart; test me and know my anxious thoughts." (Psalms 139:23)

Remember--- they may be wounded more than you know, and their lashing out at you in a non-sensitive way is just a cover up of their true feelings in their inner man!

Trust Me, I will purge them from their hurts and their feelings of *no self worth*, and love them back into the fold!

ABBA   12-12-79

THE DAY OF WINE AND ROSES

1 Cor. 3:1-3

198

Brothers, I could not address you as spiritual but as worldly--mere infants in Christ. I gave you milk, not solid food, for you were not yet ready for it. Indeed, you are still not ready. You are still worldly. For since there is jealousy and quarreling among you, are you not worldly? Are you not acting like mere men?

The day of earthly pleasures is soon to come to an end for My errant children, those children who have decided to '*live and laugh*'---just live, and heap upon themselves the treasures of this earth.

They choose to disregard Me with no acknowledgement of My existence. And... by their own unruly hands---suffer the loss of eternal peace, grace, and worship in My presence! That is not My choice. That is not My Will. For My heart's desire is that all would come to repentance and know Me. [2 Pet 3:9]

Woe to them on that day, when I come to gather My own; and they are left out of the Ark!

ABBA

THE FORMER AND LATTER RAIN

Hosea 6:3 (NKV)
Then shall we know, if we follow on to know the Lord: His going forth is prepared as the morning; and He shall come to us as the rain, as the latter and former rain unto the earth.

You took my place so that I could see the "former and latter rain." You are the one that all acclaim! For though I lie buried in a sea of sin---only the Savior has the key to open my heart and come in, filling my heart with love!

199

Only you can say, "Peace be still. I calm your waters just now." You only Lord have the power to 'till the soil,' (heart) and prepare it well---ready for seeds *of* plenty--- seeds of grace---seeds of love: love for man---to be turned into the newly plowed soil of mankind, set free by the fiery flame of your being lord!

My son is ready to repel; always ready when man rebels. He (Adam) was given dominion over all things in a day. He gave him dominion when He heard Me say, "Till the soil and name the flocks." For into your hands this day, I have placed you in charge of all things on earth.

Dear Lord and Savior of My soul I repent of my past and present misdeeds. I ---this day, give up my right to self. Live your life through me. Let not a day go by that I am reminded of Your eternal Word to praise and thank you for residing within me.

Like Adam of old, never let me forget the responsibility to care for and keep the land as you intended, passing the responsibility on to future generations until you return to take your bride home!

Help me to be so invisible in my walk with You---that only You can be seen---by those who cross My path; for You and You alone demand perfection. I will---by Your grace---wait on You as You make me to increase in working towards that goal by *being patient*, with resolve and execution of your Word, by soaking in Your "love letter to all mankind."

O, set me free this day, by your *future and latter rain*, dear Lord. ---Set me free to do Your *will*.

Blessed child of My heart---this prayer sent to my listening ears---feeds and Glorifies Me!

ABBA

THE GRAPES ARE RIPE FOR PICKING

Matthew 26:29
But I say to you, I will not drink, from now, of this fruit of the vine, until that day when I drink it new with you in my Father's kingdom.

Who are the *'grapes'* that are ready for picking, My child, do you know? They, dear heart, are the ones *steeped* in the *Word* but who have not left the pages of My hallowed book to bring forth the fruit of the vine into the *market place* for distribution; yes, they are ripe for turning the written Word *into action* for Me.

I call you to the task of opening the depth of its meaning, along with *wise council* to the 'grapes' I set before you for your care and keeping.

Anoint them with the "oil of gladness"* for active service as I continue to anoint *you* into a deeper understanding of the "fenced in, and hidden things."

Always be ready to direct the paths of those who set out to do My bidding; no small task that I call you to, O Son, O Daughter, who are called by My name and are part of the *unrelenting team*---fit for the Master's use!

Encourage the *ripened grape,* now released for *unlimited service* in *My name*, seeking out the who-so-ever-wills that cross their path, teaching, and sharing the *Word of Life Everlasting*...as they, in turn, seek out more and more *grapes* ripe for picking.

Be ever faithful to your calling in Me!

ABBA

*Hebrews 1:9

You have loved righteousness and hated wickedness; therefore God, your God, has set you above your companions by anointing you with the oil of joy.

Jeremiah 33:3
Call to me and I will answer you and tell you great and unsearchable things you do not know.

THE HEARING EAR AND
THE SEEING EYE

Proverbs 20:12
Ears that hear and eyes that see-- the LORD has made them both.

"O! Lord---Your Heavenly Kingdom, which we, your children, *long for* seems, at times, so far off as we view it in this *world of pain*. Yet, by faith and trust in Your Word, our hearing ear and seeing eye are a personal reality to those of us that intimately *know You*. We sense Your ever-present guiding Hand in this *'mission field'* here on earth.

Tell us daily, O Lord, as you did David of old, [Ps. 5:8] clearly what you would have us do and which way you would have us turn!

We are Your vessels guided by Your hand as You remind us daily: "This is the way---walk you in it!"

ABBA

Isaiah 30:21
Whether you turn to the right or to the left, your ears will hear a voice behind you, saying, "This is the way; walk in it."

THE LORD OF THE MOMENTS

Acts 2:2
Suddenly a sound like the blowing of a violent wind came from heaven and filled the whole house where they were sitting.

I Am the God of order---the most High God---Holy and true!

The message this day reflects a word given to: "Two listeners" of My *whispered voice.* I said that, "I was the lord of the moments, creator of the snow drops and the mighty oak."

This---My children holds true in this your day!

You battle against the circumstances that bring *contrary winds* to your doorstep. Fret not---I am in *every moment of your dilemmas* ---and your joys.

Why do I allow *contrary winds*---yes---even gentle ones to cross My beloved's path? Dear ones, I know your frame---and I know what is in man! (Jn. 2:25)

I give him *freedom within limits* to keep him or her on track. "In this world you will have tribulation." (Mt. 24:21) Since the *'fall'* all mankind has been afflicted with *man-made* pressures as well as satanic darts fired at you with the intent to wound---bring fear----or *kill out right*, making you ineffective for the Kingdom's work to bring common man into *My haven of rest* as they, through you, confess that Jesus Christ is the *Lord of their lives!*

Know that you who have committed to My way---you who have given Me your hearts and wills, that I am with you to *comfort, lead* and *guide you* in *the Way.*

Loved one, until you receive this message *down deep* in your being---assured, by faith, that it is so---you will never sense 'communion rest' *in Me!*

O why do you tarry? Why do you bare the scars of your own fears and unbelief? Until you experience Me as El Shaddai ---(Heb. El Elyon) ("God Most High")--- you will continue to suffer *moment by moment* ---refusing to acknowledge Me as *the lord of all your moments.*

ABBA

Genesis 14:20
And blessed be God Most High, who delivered your enemies into your hand...

2 Cor. 4:7
But we have this treasure in jars of clay to show that this all-surpassing power is from God and not from us.

THE LORD'S SUPPER

1 Cor. 11:23-25
For I received from the Lord what I also passed on to you: The Lord Jesus, on the night he was betrayed, took bread, and when he had given thanks, he broke it and said, "This is my body, which is for you; do this in remembrance of me." In the same way, after supper he took the cup, saying, "This cup is the new covenant in my blood; do this, whenever you drink it, in remembrance of me."

Examine yourself *first*, before you partake of My Body and Blood. Do not hurry---but pause and reflect! I even I, bring into your remembrance things that have been buried deep in your soul.

Then---in obedience---let the *fruit of repentance* speak forth from your lips to My listening ear, and I will make you as clean as freshly driven snow.

Then---My *cleansed* one---partake of My Body and Blood in remembrance of the price I paid to bring you back into harmony with My father and yours!

Carry on O! Forgiven one, and enter into the joy of the Lord, fully prepared for your next assignment.

Take heart---you are never alone, when in service to Me; for My warrior angels walk in front and in back of you as you carry on in the task of bringing yet one or more souls to the foot of My throne, and you will hear me say to your listening ear: Well done, O good and faithful servant, ---well done. Enter now into the joy of your Lord!

ABBA   7-12-09

THE MINISTRY OF COMPASSION

2 Chron. 36:15
    The LORD, the God of their fathers, sent word to them through his messengers again and again, because he had pity on his people and on his dwelling place.

Who will go? Who will stay? We will say, "You are loved, we care. We will pray. We will seek God even in tears to aid your release from bondage."

So many, so many that cannot find the door. "There are no handles," they say, "How are we to know the way?"

Deluded ones out for fun. Deluded ones taking up the gun. If they only knew how *thin the thread* is that holds it all together.

A violent windstorm, a rumble in the sea will bring them to their knees. Dull of hearing within My camp stifles the chant that could bring about change.

Your mission call still rings true---your mission soon coming out of the blue (quickly). So many ruts in the road, like many valleys along a narrow way. No vehicle can travel there without the driver experiencing despair.

"But enough I say, enough." My own are tough and strong in their spirit. My children are rough, even to the shaking of the soul and spirit of those too lame to call for help, but help is on the way!

Seek out---seek out by prayer and praise, others like you who will take up the challenge, and pray forth a blessing so big…so bold that will bring them into the fold!

ABBA   9-12-82

THE NEVER FAILING GOD

Hebrews 13:5

> Keep your lives free from the love of money and be content with what you have, because God has said, "Never will I leave you; never will I forsake you."

How appropriate. For He said, "I will never leave you nor forsake you." That, My dear ones, is comforting to know.

Yes! Even when all of hell is breaking in---and around you! Even in your most anxious times as you ask Me, "Couldn't things go along better, My Lord? Couldn't the pressures, lessen?"

My child---the cares of this world indeed reach out to ensnare, trap, and try to render you helpless---in a sea of despairing circumstances.

But---loved one, Jesus is more than you know---more than your soul and mind can comprehend!

You know, by faith and trust alone, that He is faithful and will not allow you to take more than you can bear.

To all those who have *given over* to Me their *will*, for My care and keeping in trust,----I give you insight into My heavenly plan for you---one day at a time; for that is all you need to know!

I AM your guide and stay; I chart the path ahead of you, and tell you *where to stop* and rest. (Psalm 139:3) (Liv)

Stay in the Word---read, praise, and praise Me; for I inhabit the praises of My children. Individual lives unfold when you are subjected to the *pressure cooker* of life!

The Lord, in His perfect timing---will remove all the barriers of life that now confront you and will make *a way in the wilderness.*

Your position in Him is that *you be found faithful*, and the Holy Spirit ---Himself, will chart, and control your course!

ABBA   7-12-09

THE NEW DISPERSION

Isaiah 11:11

In that day the Lord will reach out his hand a second time to reclaim the remnant that is left of his people from Assyria, from Lower Egypt, from Upper Egypt, from Cush, from Elam, from Babylonia, from Hamath and from the islands of the sea.

Whose hand rests upon the wheel of conversion? Is it those of the dispersion? Those whose hearts have been turned in the direction of the Author and Giver of life?

Whose hands rest upon the wheel of conversion? Is it those mighty with pen as sharp as a sword--- Mighty with an educated span of the word---in chapter form? Or is it the hand of those whose inner man has forged within that consecrated one the desire, zeal, and the vision of the heavenly task at hand?

For the hand that rests upon the wheel of conversion is steady---one whose heart has been set as flint---One who has committed with singleness of heart to press on in Him, despite earthly claims upon his time, talents or monetary gain.

For you of the New Dispersion, set your cap for even the weakest cry for help--- cast in My direction. In love ferret them out, for your desire is for Me. Reach out to those in need---turn their hearts in the direction of Him which calls, who sanctifies, who justifies---who eternally cries, "Rest your hand—even now on that wheel of conversion---and follow My lead!"

ABBA

THE PLANE OF YOUR IMAGINATIONS

Jeremiah 23:17

They keep saying to those who despise me, 'The LORD says: You will have peace.' And to all who follow the stubbornness of their hearts they say, 'No harm will come to you.'

What is next upon the plane (level) of your imaginations? Time to take stock---time to search out the people---places---situations, and their circumstances. Time to weave them into action.

Time to move along the path that will lead them to My throne room. Sort out the *'wheat* from the tares' (a noxious weed) and get them (wheat) started in the knowledge of Me!

Then move up and out, through your family ties and friends alike. They have eyes, help them to see Me---see them involved in small groups, where those in the group have walked with Me, past dining on the *milk of the Word* and growing along the path toward maturity, adding the babes just learning to eat the *meat of the Word*!

See them waiting and longing for Me. Dwell on places visited---near and far. Brood *(think deeply)* over them, like a mother hen broods over her newborn chicks!

Be an example to them in thought, word, and deed. Help them to love each other, giving them a *new balance* as they continue to learn more and more of Me.

Help them learn to receive and give joy and glory to the Father, Son, and Holy Spirit.

Do you find some in *dire circumstances*, running against the wind? What is in your hands and heart that will make a difference in their lives? (Eccles. 9:10)

Do they need a 'course-correction'---or are you finding some, *lazily adrift* and off My path. Help them to quickly make the correction when you find them running against the wind in their lives.

I have called you to this task---arise, take your time. Do all things in an orderly fashion, things that are necessary to return some to the fold--- those who are beginning to stray off the course. Because--- dear ones---you have learned to praise and pray, I have launched you deeper into My work!

*Eccles. 9:10

Whatever your hand finds to do, do it with all your might, for in the grave, where you are going, there is neither working nor planning nor knowledge nor wisdom.

THE POT IS BOILING

Matthew 25:32

All the nations will be gathered before him, and he will separate the people one from another as a shepherd separates the sheep from the goats.

The pot is boiling within each person you pray for. Every pot is filled with liquids of *each one's choosing.*

Steam is being released from their pots, all with *different flavors.* Some are sweet smelling to the nostrils; others have a putrid, rank, distasteful odor belching forth--- even to the *contamination of others!*

I AM, by My own right hand, separating the stench from the *sweet released steam.*

As you pray. . .as you give Me praise, as your concerned prayers are released . . .racing skyward toward My Throne, I, yes, I, will release the sweet aroma from their pots to *touch others* for good until all the steam from every pot you prayed for brings forth . . . *sweetness* only!

ABBA   *5-8-03*

THE POWER AND AUTHORITY

Matthew 9:6

But so that you may know that the Son of Man has authority on earth to forgive sins . . ." Then he said to the paralytic, "Get up, take your mat and go home."

Luke 4:36
All the people were amazed and said to each other, "What is this teaching? With authority and power he gives orders to evil spirits and they come out!"

I have given you, when in obedience to Me, the *authority* and *power*---using My name ---to demand the evil one to leave you and return from whence he come.

Claim the blood of Jesus over you, as you stand fully armed for battle. Stand and watch Me scatter the enemy on your behalf.

Take heed to these words, precious ones. Repent when you fall. Failure to do this puts you in danger of having your *lampstand* removed.

ABBA   10-09-80

Rev. 2:5
Remember the height from which you have fallen! Repent and do the things you did at first. If you do not repent, I will come to you and remove your lampstand from its place.

THE RAGING STORM WITHIN

Mark 4:37-41
A furious squall came up, and the waves broke over the boat, so that it was nearly swamped. Jesus

was in the stern, sleeping on a cushion. The disciples woke him and said to him, "Teacher, don't you care if we drown?" He got up, rebuked the wind and said to the waves, "Quiet! Be still!" Then the wind died down and it was completely calm. He said to his disciples, "Why are you so afraid? Do you still have no faith?" They were terrified and asked each other, "Who is this? Even the wind and the waves obey him!"

Do you reside in a great harbor---content to rest among the shoals (shallows)? Are you content to reside in that great harbor, moored in safety; is your greatest test---fighting ripples that lap against your stern?

Or are you able to *break the chains that bind you*? Are you filled with the promises of God? Are you able to launch out beyond the breakwaters of life, daring to stand in the fullness of your faith, atop of the *cresting waves*; for My waves do not crest before reaching the shore.

Like an ever-rolling tide, with furious, unleashed powers churning the very waters of the sea. Can you ---in Me, rise above the fury and rescue that drowning one, caught up in the ravages of life----those storm tossed *water-logged* souls in complete disrepair?

Are you able to stand astride the crest with eyes on the *goal of life*? Can you concentrate on His overcoming presence, hand in hand, and feel His power course through your being?

From His hand to yours---with your hand stretched forth to others, sensing His power and glory---are you able to be let loose upon the waters of life?

In Him is no striving. In Him is no bewilderment. In Him is no defeat---even for you who dare to leave the safety of that *untroubled water in the harbor*—just trusting His hand!

Your very angel will place your feet upon those angry waves---and head you out to the sea, free of a storm filled life. So---My child, put on the full armor of God and see the salvation of the Lord in action.

Stand and watch earthly temples fall before His majestic hands, for He is more than able to calm the raging storm within the breast of man. He is able to receive that child who is in *restraint* (checking their true feelings) when talking with others, free from His man-made harbor of safety.

Let us go forth in the knowledge of Him who came--- putting an end to sickness and death. Let the winds blow. Let the storms arise. We stand in the presence of the Master, O child of My heart---what more do you need --- but Me!

ABBA   6-8-88

THE REFINING STILL GOES ON

Malachi 3:3
> He will sit as a refiner and purifier of silver; he will purify the Levites and refine them like gold and silver. Then the LORD will have men who will bring offerings in righteousness.

The refining still goes on. You need the blessing of My relentless pressure. You are learning to abide the heat; for out of the very fires of affliction, I bring the 'former and latter rain.' (Jer. 5:24)

Help the babes in Me to endure as they grow into maturity. Join with those in like accord. Seek to band together from time to time to remove the obstacles in the

213

children's way until they are able to *eat meat,* and are able to aid in the defeat of that fallen foe.

Note your daily life; it should be clearly of My design. Always strive to be in the center of My *will.*

There are myriads *who will be saved.* We still have time; it is on our side. Rest now in the peace of the Lord.

ABBA   5-24-80

THE RELATIONSHIP OF BELIEVERS

John 15:12-13
My command is this: Love each other as I have loved you. Greater love has no one than this, that he lay down his life for his friends.

In this world you will have trials and tribulation; but I know My own, and they, in turn, take good care of one another, especially looking after the widows and the infirm and those who have fallen upon hard times... in their midst and sphere of influence.

To you who are recently widowed---do not stay away from the church assembly; you will find many who will love and support you in your grief.

You will find others who have been widowed for some time; draw strength from them as they get on with their lives and continue to serve Me well!

Take care of those who have fallen upon hard times financially. Serve them as you would serve Me, and they in turn should receive your gifts of time and talents gracefully!

The bond of believers is akin to your own immediate family members, who rejoice and pray for you in your time of need---supporting you in every way.

For the time will come when you all will grace My table of love as royalty begets royalty in My kingdom.

To those that the father has given Me---I have given to them that they may be glorified; for I have passed My glory on to them, also, to serve Me by sharing the kingdom of heaven throughout the world.

Let that special anointing be on them as your *light* in them is seen by all with whom they come in contact... as your aroma, O Father, is passed on through them to a heart sick people--- when they meet and share the good news of the gospel to the who-so-ever-wills that cross their path.

May the body of Christ multiply one hundred fold, as they seek out and cause people to be saved---as they gather together as one, in power, and praise your name, spreading the gospel of Jesus' love for all mankind!

ABBA   8-14-09

THE SAINTS AND THE SEEDLINGS

Eph. 1:17-18

I keep asking that the God of our Lord Jesus Christ, the glorious Father, may give you the Spirit of wisdom and revelation, so that you may know him better. I pray also that the eyes of your heart may be enlightened in order that you may know the hope to which he has called you, the riches of his glorious inheritance in the saints...

Think about this: 'How does one go about distinguishing between the *saints and the seedlings?*

(Prov. 4:7) Wisdom is supreme; therefore get wisdom. Though it cost all you have, get understanding.

"My mouth shall speak wisdom, and the meditation of my heart---shall give understanding." (Ps. 49:3) Grow in grace and knowledge of our Lord and Savior Jesus Christ.

Digest these thoughts, loved ones. Live and breathe these instructions---and, My dears, you will be well fortified and grounded in the word,

Now---after having embraced these truths, seek the seedlings! Who are the seedlings? (Mt. 13:19) They are those who hear the words of the kingdom and do not understand; the enemy---Satan, snatches away what was sewn in their hearts by the *wayside*. (Mt. 13: 20-21) The words of truth fell on stony places. These, reseed.

Others are those who hear the word and immediately receive it with joy---but they have no *root* in their lives (little or no understanding of what is being said)---soon tribulation or persecution arises because of the word and they stumble!

O! Child of My kingdom, draw these seedlings to your bosom. Nurture them, and pour out your love into their confused hearts of despair.

Love them into the wisdom, understanding, and knowledge of your Lord and Savior-- Jesus the anointed one!

You will have done a great mizspah (good deed).

ABBA

THE SECRET OF GOD GIVEN WEALTH

Luke 6:38

Give, and it will be given unto you. A good measure, pressed down, shaken together, and running over, will be poured into your lap. For with the measure you use, it will be measured to you.

How to use your wealth in service to Me!

Finances used wisely, open vistas (as seen through a long passage of opportunities) to serve My purposes, through you, O child of My heart, to use in service to Me!

I will give you hidden riches.* Hoarded finances reduce you to a life of missed opportunities to give to your fellow man, who is in desperate need at times.

I caution you that ill-gotten gains, by whatever means, *legal* thievery, for example, will be judged and punished by whatever methods I choose!

Freely you have been given, freely give *in all ways*. Heal the sick, raise the walking dead, cleans the lepers, cast out demons.

Now--give your time and your talents, which is also the *true path of giving*; and I will bless you in ways of loving service that you do not know!

Call on Me, and I will answer you and I will tell you great and mighty things, fenced in things---hidden things that you do not know!

The greatest wealth of all is to know Me, and that I abide (remain) in you! (1Jn. 3:24)

So dear hearts---be off on any mission I assign to you; and whatever your hands find to do, whether giving of your finances or service, do it with all your might! (Eccl. 9:10)

ABBA   11-14-09

Isaiah 45:3

I will give you the treasures of darkness, riches stored in secret places, so that you may know that I am the LORD, the God of Israel, who summons you by name.

217

THE WORLD IS IN NEED OF CLEANSING

Psalm 51:2
Wash me thoroughly from my iniquity, and
cleanse me from my sin.

This broken world is in need of cleansing. You, O repented one, can and must, when guided by My hand, bring about change.

Now loved one---stand tall in Me. Straighten out your armor and bring it to a dress-parade polish. Walk on in the light of My Word. Read and praise Me more. Above all--- be always in an attitude of prayer.

When you fall---even over the slightest thing that brings disharmony to you and others---quickly repent and walk on.

Keep in mind that this earth you walk on is full of *mine fields*. Look to Me in prayer with patience, and I will lead you safely around them.

Quiet yourself now. Sense My healing ointment upon you and walk on in service to Me---O forgiven sinner.

ABBA   10-5-80

THERE IS A DAY COMING SOON

Mark 9:1
And he said to them, "I tell you the truth, some who are standing here will not taste death before they see the kingdom of God come with power."

There is a day coming soon when the tides of battle will shift, and the Heavenly battle will *dip down to you.* Are you prepared---are you ready to stand with Me forming the *wall,* giving comfort to all who fall?

No harm will befall you as you take your stand. You are guarded and loved. I have so few who will be My hands and feet, in love retuning the lost and strayed to Me.

For just one *dedicated saint,* firmly concentrating on Me, expands him or herself in service to Me. Soon they, those wicked ones, will see---that Jesus still walks, through you, the barren land laid waste by war, looking for those in search of Godly love ---giving aid to all---slave or free...Wooing them back to My eternal tree!

Your spirits have been awakened, O faithful ones. You have been obedient to listen for My voice with your inner ear, reading and praying. So I bring you closer to the fray. Others too I AM bringing along.

Be firm---be stable---and you will see that I enlarge your tents, lengthening your cords and strengthening your stakes.*

The lines are now firmly drawn---the enemy defined. Get your armor ready---and be suited up. I now position you next to Me, and we walk on, you and I, toward that heavenly goal.

But first—we must pause along the way, as I ready you for battle, and let you fight the *important*---but *little wars! The massive ones,* beloved, *leave them to Me!*

ABBA

*Isaiah 54:2

Enlarge the place of your tent, stretch your tent curtains wide, do not hold back; lengthen your cords, strengthen your stakes.

THERE IS NO HIGHER CALLING

Matthew 22:14
"For many are invited, but few are chosen."

You have been chosen from your mother's womb (Is. 49:1) to serve Me all the days of your life. I honor you for not only choosing to give Me your *will*, but also continuing to be that witness for all to see and follow in your dedication to Me!

There isn't a day or night goes by that you, with My help, walk, talk, and mirror My son in thought word and deed.

There awaits you a glorious place of rest and eternal activity in My kingdom---along with all your family and friends alike that have gone on before you!

Even your *seed* (Gen. 22.17-18) continues to follow in your footsteps; for you have been their guide and stay these many years.

You continue to bear *much fruit* (Jn.15:8) and have continued to bless and praise Me; for indeed. "I inhabit the praises of My children!"

You have humbled yourself to serve mankind in service to Me (Ps. 34:2) in your church, among your friends and small groups, and to *exalt* the name of Christ before all the who-so-ever-wills, that are so eager to learn about My Son!

For this I bless you. You, like king David of old, are a man after God's own heart. Continue to proclaim Jesus in word and deed!

ABBA   9-14-09

THIRSTY COME TO THE WATER AND DRINK

Rev. 7:16
Never again will they hunger; never again will they thirst. The sun will not beat upon them, nor any scorching heat.

Come to the water all you are thirsty and drink. For I AM that pure fountain---My springs run deep ---refined to perfection.

Where is that man, women or child, who longs to drink from My well? Where is that band of believing saints--- starved for a cup of cool clear water from that fountain of love?

Where are those, going about the business of their daily lives, who will stop and drink to the dregs---that portion of living water held in reserve for them---daily?

Who can know the anguish of My heart? Who can know My pain, watching My creation in travail?

I would that any man, thirsty or not, be receptive to My available waters! But man in his conscious freedom, has for the most part, ignored the "streams in the desert"---that which is able to free-up his inner man.

---That which is able to open his understanding--- releasing his inner ear to hear My eternal instructions and whisperings of love from My flaming heart!

O! Come to the *water of redemption*, and be cleansed! Come to the *water of life* and live!

Purify your hearts---come, wash yourselves in the *hollow of My hand.* Turn ---turn today---for today is the day of *new beginnings*---Today is the first day of your *new life!*

Note the righteous man---for his way is the way of peace! Note that righteous woman---for her ways are

221

known to Me. Mark and shun the evil man---the greedy man---for they are caught-up in worldly affairs that dishonor My name.

O! Child of wrath and pain---turn to the fountain of love! I eagerly pray to the Father in your behalf, coming against the enemy of your soul. Turn and live---turn and read---turn and pray---turn, in your joyous wonder---to the God of the universe----and praise Him---the author and finisher of your faith!

ABBA

THIS IS THE WAY WALK IN IT

Isa. 30:21
Whether you turn to the right or to the left, your ears will hear a voice behind you, saying, "This is the way; walk in it."

O! Lord, I have turned my head to the right and to the left this day, and know not what I should do next. Tell me clearly what to do today and which way to turn. (Ps. 5:8)

I have been to the heights of Zion and also to the depths of 'no-man's' land; yet I know not to trust my feelings of despair but to trust only your guiding hand, day by day and minute by minute. I know by believing faith and trust that You are closer to me than a brother.

Seek My face, O child of My heart; for I bear all your feelings of loneliness. I bring you out of the depths of despair.

Ever know that I Am your sure strong anchor. Yes! The world is in turmoil, and the heathens that now run your government attempt to disregard---your nation's "God given right" to make your own choices without government intervention!

But fear not; I brought forth your nation to secure freedom from narcissistic people in high places, those who work unrighteousness amongst your fellow man. Know that I work for those who wait for Me.

Yes, you see those in power trying to destroy this nation's constitution; but remember, "The battle is not yours---but mine."

Follow Me; for this is the way---walk you in it!

ABBA   10-31-09

THIS NEW PLACE OF REST

Hebrews 4:8-11

...For if Joshua had given them rest, God would not have spoken later about another day. There remains, then, a Sabbath-rest for the people of God; for anyone who enters God's rest also rests from his own work, just as God did from his. Let us, therefore, make every effort to enter that rest, so that no one will fall by following their example of disobedience.

My children's greatest sin is not knowing or understanding the word *rest*; this is one of Satan's tools to keep My children on the run---rushing along through life without enjoying My wide range of creativeness!

I would caution all who read this message to take the time to see Me in all of My creations, some hidden beyond their senses in their earthly surroundings.

Look deep into every living plant, bush and landscape; note the various colors and the look of all of nature.

223

Loved ones---this is how I have made human beings; all so unique that even they are not truly aware of their own individualisms!

I died for each and every one of you---past or present, and will continue to watch over My flock until the day of My choosing to bring all those who are going to be saved to an end, saved and ready to come home to My everlasting kingdom---enjoying Me face to face!

It will not be long, beloved ones, as I look down from above and see reenacted before My eyes---Sodom and Gomorrah revisited on this generation, who are so taken with all of life's pleasures in the *here and now*---with no thought of Me.   Lust and permissiveness reign with complete disregard for another's feelings---all in the name of money, and power over mankind!

Watch, dear ones of My personal flock, watch for the signs of the times, and learn to rely on all My promises, which are conditional on obedience and a lifestyle of repentance.

A final warning: When you fall away under any kind of pressure, whether from man or non-avoidable situations, do not fall for Satan's words, "Has God said?"   Be quick to ask in faith and believing trust for forgiveness.

Please note, beloveds, that I have put those sins behind Me and remember them no more!

ABBA   7-20-09

THOSE WHO WOULD FOLLOW ME

Rev. 14:4

These are those who did not defile themselves with women, for they kept themselves pure. They follow the Lamb wherever he goes. They were purchased from among men and offered as firstfruits to God and the Lamb.

Those who would follow Me, take heed. This is no luxury trip. Stop and count the cost! Would you follow Me in near and faraway places?

Would you take-up your cross, day after day and walk in trust, totally given over to My demands and commands? Trust Me without seeing up ahead? *Holding nothing back?*

I look for those who have bent their hearts to read, pray, and praise My name, their 'chief corner stone,' every day to enter the fray---counting the cost!

I AM their pathfinder---only I know the plans that I have for you---plans for good and not for evil, to give you a future and a hope! (Jer. 29:11-12)

You are that chosen few---the remnant that have thrown all caution to the wind to follow Me!.

I know what lies ahead of everyone who has counted the cost--and abandonment required---to do My bidding.

Yes! What I have tasked you to do daily is to take up your *sword and follow Me. There are people desperately waiting to be released from their own self-made prisons---people who have lost their way. People----who have made it this far on their own—but unknowingly have ended up in a blind alley. Their well-laid plans have ended up at in a *sudden dead end!*

Help them to turn their lives around---as they, through you, learn of Me and the plans I have for their lives.

Some have come to Me in their later years---bruised, beaten, and broken.

Open their eyes to the Light of this world: Jesus, My son, who can take away their *misspent lives*, walking up and down looking for peace and prosperity.

I the 'hound of heaven'—have waited for them to give up their earthly plans for fame and fortune, and now to realize that all their self-made plans were nothing more than *smoke and mirrors.* Pick them up and tenderly bring them back to their senses.

Show them---by your example of love for them---that I AM the Truth and the Way (John 14:6). Only I can rebuild their lives, if at first, they give Me their *will* without reservation; and I will take back the lost years that the "canker worm has eaten."

Restore them to a life filled with righteousness, peace and joy in the Holy Spirit. The Holy Spirit will guide you in their restoration from hell itself.

Set them on the path of fellowship with others who have cast their lot in Me.

O the joy and inner peace that will follow them and will know no bounds! As they trust and obey, taking access to all My promises, I will answer all their deep needs, not only their wants; if they will live a lifestyle of obedience and repentance.

O the joy that will come to their inner man---when they will hear Me say, "Well done, good and faithful servant, enter into the joy of your Lord!"

I say again, "Come now and enter the eternal peace and love of your Lord and master!"

ABBA   6-24-09

*Eph. 6:17
Take the helmet of salvation and the sword of the Spirit, which is the word of God:

THREE FOUNDATIONAL ANCHORS
TO YOUR FAITH

CHARACTER	STRENGTH	CHALLENGE
Daniel	Sampson	St. Paul
Dan. 6:31	Judges 16:3	Acts 9:15-16

I have chosen the writer of this message to pick up his pen and show you, who dare to follow Me all the days of your lives—beloveds.

These are the three *core values* for you to build into your inner man:

CHARACTER: Daniel
Against all odds after he was deported to Babylon at the age of sixteen and hand picked for government service, he became My prophetic mouthpiece to the Gentile and Jewish world, declaring My present and eternal purpose.
.... "READ AND OBEY"

STRENGTH: Samson
Now Sampson at midnight arose and took hold of the doors of the city gate and the two posts. He pulled them up along with the bars; then he put them on his shoulders and carried them up to the *top of the mountain.*
.... "READ AND OBEY"

CHALLENGE: Apostle Paul
The Lord says, "Go for he is a chosen instrument of Mine, to bear My name before the Gentiles, kings and sons of

Israel; for I will show him *how much he must suffer for My names sake.*

.... "READ AND PRAY"

Consider these three, beloveds, especially in the days ahead of you. Build into your *inner man* the three lives above who gave their all for Me and serve as an example of the three core values you must acquire to *stay the course* and be My witness as you live your dedicated lives before all of mankind!

If you can stay the course, and it will not be easy, My Spirit will guard your paths to bring all the who-so-ever-wills into the kingdom of righteousness, peace, and joy in the Holy Spirit.

ABBA   10-25-09

TIMES OF TESTING

Exodus 20:20
    Moses said to the people, "Do not be afraid. God has come to test you, so that the fear of God will be with you to keep you from sinning."

Why do you strive in your own power to know My plan, and then *doubt* the direction I take you in? Don't attempt to erase those troubled circumstances you find yourself in?

Know this---I am in *all* your circumstances! O! Don't you realize that these times of testing are brought to show you that I care for you in a very special way.

Don't wonder at My silence, but spend time in My book for it is all laid out for you in My Word. Wait for the power of the Holy Spirit to intervene in your behalf.

I sit on your side of the grandstand, supporting your efforts to grow in Me---another foot---another yard until that day when I say, " It is enough---come home to Me *now,* loved one; all is made ready for your arrival! "

ABBA

TO THE VICTOR BELONG THE SPOILS

1 John 5:4
...for everyone born of God overcomes the world. This is the victory that has overcome the world, even our faith.

To the victor belong the spoils---To the victor. It is he---it is she, who has toiled and struggled---who has reached the higher ground.

Drained and purified by the blood of the Lamb---strained through the *grist wheel of time.*

Behold---the Light---behold ---the Man!

Grand and glorious is the stature of this one. Yes, you see only the shadow of Him (Jesus)---the light about His frame presents a perfect silhouette.

Be still my heart; be still! Lift your heart and eyes---let them pour over this silhouetted form, arms reaching out to enfold the world!

To the victor belong the spoils. *Know* now by prayer and praise lifted to My ears, that your victory is assured. *Know,* by His shadowed presence, as He stands tall and serene upon His mountaintop, that He sees into the valleys of the hearts of man.

Know that His lighted sword pierces the darkness of the soul of man. *Know* that His surgery is complete---by the letting of His blood!

Know, O victorious one, that you are complete, and need not know defeat---in Him. *Know* that His thoughts are constantly upon the children of His first love!

Know that He weeps, as should you, for the hearts of the unsaved! Finally My beloveds...

Know victory, My sweet; know victory. ----You have *gained the spoil*---the 'pearl of great price' "Jesus." You have gained even Him!

Speak the praises of the Lord. Let all flesh bless His Holy name!

ABBA   10-5-89

TO WHOM CAN YOU COMPARE

Isaiah 46:5

"To whom will you compare me or count me equal? To whom will you liken me that we may be compared?

Compared to the battle where the enemy is openly rampant; compared to the battle, where the blood is beaten out of the backs of those made in the image of Me.

Compared to the battlefields where the maimed and fear ridden ones lie are the *gifts of servitude---dedication---forbearance---patience---- trust and long suffering* along with the *peace in the inner man.*

The gifts I have given My servants today ease the pain of the battles, real or imagined. Won back for Me, by their repentance and re-dedication, I take *in trust,* removing the *coated scales from their eyes.*

I see you battling alone, in the open field when you take them on. I see you looking around as you flay your hands about, *warding off the darts,* looking for the dust of one or more dedicated men, scurrying towards you, at your given command, forming a wall of protection about you to defend the poor---wretched and blind---caught-up and ravaged by the continuing battle in this earthly realm---as you and yours thresh about, seeing the evil ones---now touching down where you live and toil---beginning their rampage!

These foul spirits squeal and shout, knowing that their days are numbered, as you call upon My name, while using *intercessory prayer* for the outnumbered ones caught up in the fray; this tips the scales as the war soars on, touching down into this country.

The rest of the world sits and gazes as if it were in a theatre watching a play, wringing their hands and saying, "How awful, how awful." But do they enter the conflict? Why no--of course not! They think it a contest upon the stage, set back in time, away from the fray. Why they *hardly take the time to pray!*

But, suddenly the battle strikes them---in their very *heartland. Hundreds,* nay, *thousands* are suddenly swept into eternity---without a word or whimper (some are *saved* some *are not).*

There is none like Me *(Ex. 8:10) I hear the murmurings of the children. "O take and eat," and you shall be filled with bread; in spite of the battles, in spite of the uncertainties, continue to *till your lands*---and make them fruitful---until I come! You are made in My image---be strengthened in the inner man. Put on your armor daily (*the Word of God*) go out among them. Take courage, you walk not alone *(Heb. 13:5-6).*

To whom can you compare Me? I and I alone hold you in the palm of My hand. Yes---suffering comes in this broken world---but *I have overcome the world.* Put your trust in My name: In the Name above all names. By My name you can rout the foul spirits---sending them back to the pits of hell itself.

Those who are Mine hear My voice and take on the authority and power of My son himself!

Go now and do battle---*in My name.*

ABBA

*Exodus 8:10

"Tomorrow," Pharaoh said. Moses replied, "It will be as you say, so that you may know there is no one like the LORD our God.

*Hebrews 13:5-6

Keep your lives free from the love of money and be content with what you have, because God has said, "Never will I leave you; never will I forsake you." So we say with confidence, "The Lord is my helper; I will not be afraid. What can man do to me?"

TRANSFERING ELIJAH'S MANTLE

2 Cor. 3:18

And we, who with unveiled faces all reflect the Lord's glory, are being transformed into his likeness with ever-increasing glory, which comes from the Lord, who is the Spirit.

I am, as in the days of old, transferring your beloved's mantle on to you, My son!

Be that spiritual counselor that I had gifted her to be. Delve deep into My Word; absorb the fruit that you find there by pondering, along with prayer, what I spoke to the prophets.

My Spirit and theirs met as one, passing the Word along in *written form* to others.

O! Servant of My heart, continue on as a *solid anchor*, foundationally grounded in Me as I, the 'Hound Of Heaven,' will direct your paths of connection to the who-so-ever-wills and also to your brothers and sisters in Christ.

I love you, faithful one!

ABBA   5-20-08

Author's Note: On May 15, 2008, my beloved wife Jean went home to be with the Lord.   We had 57 wonderful years together, serving the Lord as One!

TRIALS AND TRIBULATIONS

John 16:33
These things I have spoken to you, that in Me you might have peace. In the world you shall have tribulation: but be of good cheer; I have overcome the world.

Are you overwhelmed by daily trials and temptations, which are so commonplace with man, born into this broken world?

Are you troubled with what *man thinks* of you? Remember, dear one, that a man or woman's *word*---or *lack of it*---is a sure indication of the nature and character of that man or woman! Strive to be at peace with your fellow man. Serve him without reservation. You will draw to yourself that same type of person as you are.

Fellowshipping together for the cause of Christ, and whatever your hands find to do, will bring satisfaction, joy, and fulfillment to your every need!

Stand tall under fire---be that one---who, when trials and tribulations come to friends and foe alike, you can reach out in love and exhibit the love and caring of the Savior in them.

Life and people will come to you as that *solid anchor* in their lives.

Carry on until the day I call you home, always putting others first; it will attract the who-so-ever-wills to your door!

ABBA   9-30-08

*Eccles. 9:10
What ever your hand finds to do, do it with all your might...

TRIALS WILL PLAGUE YOU IN MINISTRY

2 Cor. 4:16-17
Therefore we do not lose heart. Though outwardly we are wasting away, yet inwardly we are being renewed day by day. For our light and momentary troubles are achieving for us an eternal glory that far outweighs them all.

You dare to speak out in My name and declare all that My Son came to earth to do, recovering you from the snare of the prince of this world's *misstatement*: "Has God said?"

He is the father of lies and will defeat you at every turn in your life if you are not covered by the blood of Jesus.

You can, and will, come under persecution and affliction of every known kind---from family and friends alike, who have watched you turn away from *outright sin* and every lust of the flesh---which is so common to unregenerate man.

You can look forward to being forsaken by those who still walk after sinful pleasures.

Yes! You have been struck down *at times,* but not destroyed because of the Holy Spirit, and My warrior angels, who are looking after your every need.

I AM in all your circumstance and will lead you through---and out of them---*in My timing!* As you pass through the raging fires, not a hair on your head will be scorched or burned!

Every bump in the road will be made straight, and I will lead you on to your next assignment for Me, as you seek the lost, strayed, or stolen, by the prince of this world; I will cover you with My *seamless garment* where Satan and his followers cannot penetrate.

O! Stalwart one---Keep on keeping on along the path to your eternal home---there to rest and enjoy all the activities with family and friends who have gone on before you!

Courage now, beloved, you are never alone. My angels watch over you constantly.

ABBA   8-12-09

TROUBED AND DISTURBED SHEPHERDS

2 Cor. 4:17
For our light and momentary troubles are achieving for us an eternal glory that far outweighs them all.

Out of the fires of affliction do I come! The shepherd is in need of counseling. Why do they stray---why don't they pray?

They live like strangers---in the midst of paradise. They seek to circumvent their way (avoid having to comply). These shepherds are attacked from front and oppressed from behind—filling their hours off without prayer.

The siege is on ---especially toward those who are in the first line of defense. The enemy comes ---wave after wave. Nothing new under the sun; ceaseless they come throughout every age.

Each period of man when My people align themselves with Me---the attack is relentless and is shifted to the pastor. My glory is all they seek; these are the ones who feel the heat of the battle in service to Me.

Aid your pastor and help throw out the lifeline to those who mourn and weep. Throw out the lifeline; the land is full to the bursting point with sheep in need of repair---they are in constant despair.

You, My child,---raise his standard high. Gather your council and call an assembly. The angels and the hosts of heaven are at your beck and call; they await your *directed call*.

Nothing---no task too big or small---pray forth the pastor, pray him forth to Me---until the day the Son bursts forth, and that tired shepherd---will then see that My glory will not be given to another. My glory I will not allow to be smothered.

O beloved shepherd of your precious flock, given over for your care and keeping, know that I AM in the front---I AM in the back and on each side of you---It Is Me!

Yes! I AM also at the top, and bring up the rear---I even I *fill-up the cracks! Remember*---dear shepherd of Mine---I hold the bricks together with the mortar of My Blood.

Kiss the Son (in spirit), Praise His name---never again will he be put to shame.

Remember ---you do not stand alone, O! Precious one. Your health and your life are Mine, and I use you as I will--

-I strengthen you just now. Therefore, in nothing be anxious---seek My *will*---My way is cast in cement and true.

View everything from My perspective---*view it all* from there!

ABBA

TROUBLED STORM TOSSED WATERS

Psalm 34:17
The righteous cry out, and the Lord hears them;
he delivers them from all their troubles.

Man with troubles ---cry louder. Man, *cease from sin.* Man with troubles---ponder your soul within. A portion of your breast at rest!

A portion of your breast at war---who can implore, who can say, "The man next to you is a knave." Get in tune with My Son.

Live each day as if it were your last. Bring honor to each man you meet. Bring love; for from My vantage point above I see each man's motives; I see each man's gains.

I see that man longs to bring himself---a touch of fame, a touch of class---even if he must harass another---made the same.

For in My image was man derived. For in My image, man is to survive. Man in trouble, in storm tossed waters---cry louder.

Set everything aside and concentrate on Him, concentrate on life lived in the flesh---for now. But give equal time to the Holy Spirit within.

Unbind your chains---give love to man in trouble, but not too confused. Man in trouble, all you need is your shoes;---slip them on, and trod the path of My beloved Son!

Go fishing for man—gather them up and heap them on My lap. Do all things with prayer and praise; then be off in the Spirit---be off in your mind, be off in the physical. Let a song be on your lips, let it break forth!

Man in trouble---clear your mind. Remember---remember, your struggle is not with man! The battle still rages on.

Need I remind you again---no strange thing is happening again; for we are at war against principalities, and the ravages of time---man in trouble---cry louder, say, "Jesus free me from sin today; for I repent, and would be obedient to your commands!"

"My desire is to walk within Your palatial home, on floors of gold---worshipping the Father, worshiping the Son, worshipping The Holy Spirit. Blessed three in one"!

ABBA   6-18-83

TROUBLED WATERS

Jer. 8:15
We hoped for peace but no good has come, for a time of healing but there was only terror.

How My servants toil in the midst of troubled waters!

How true My Lord---how true. Yes, my life as well as countless others have been filled with troubles. Some---our own sin filled choosing.

Others foisted upon us by the demons of hell itself, hiding within the flesh of our enemies---and they are many-

--intent on turning us into parrots of false religious (man-made)---or killing us without a trace of a tear!

You have said it rightly, My child.

In Your Book You speak of "wars and rumors of wars." (Mt. 24:6) (Mk. 13:7) In this the end time days it is more 'wars' than 'rumors' ---only You know the times and places, Lord.

In your holy wisdom---You allow it to bring man into a right relationship with your Son. For man---since the fall has determined ---by his own self-will and actions to distance himself from Your guiding hand of protection, believing that man can go it alone. God haters all, are they that decide upon this path of destruction for their existence and worldly pleasures.

But...in a twinkling of an eye---You, dear Lord, ---will bring them into account, allowing the world to beat them into its mold---until they cry out in remorse: "Abba Father--- show me the way to Your door step. Hear my cry. Open, and let me come into the warmth of Your presence, life, and fire."

Some---beyond saving, through their hardness of their hearts will never surrender your call.

Soon, I bring you out of troubled waters to enjoy peace and rest. Trust---trust Me now. That is the order of the day. Take time to delve into My Word. Drink deeply of its contents---and pray.

You were meant to fly (above the circumstances) Yes--- even to soar. Now dear child---take your rest--- in Me.

ABBA

TRUE LOVE

1 John 4:21

And he has given us this command: Whoever loves God must also love his brother.

True love is, "Seeking man's highest good." It means: What is the very best for their ultimate needs and aspirations!

Therefore---be My witness in everything you do in My name, as did I, for the lost, strayed, or stolen by Satan and his demonic forces.

I encourage you to go *that extra mile* for man; for they are so in need of realizing that *someone cares!* Give anything (within reason) to him who asks you: time, talents, or money, and do not turn away from him who wants to borrow from you. (Matt. 5:22)

I, in My love for man, gave without restraint to those in need; for I satisfy their needs (in My timing) not *their wants!* My son was the ultimate witness (while on earth) as a witness of My love---as was Paul who epitomized *'true love' serving mankind* wherever My Holy Spirit directed his paths. He went without reservation!

So you shall follow the Holy Spirit's prompting---yes even going into countries which despise the name of Christ as they ignorantly follow the false prophets of this world.

Yes! Some have paid with their lives in service to Me. That, dear ones, is *true love.* When you go through the waters of affliction, (you name the category), I will work it out to your *greatest good* beloved!

ABBA   9-21-09

TRUST HIS WAYS

Isaiah 12:2
Surely God is my salvation; I will trust and not be afraid. The LORD, the LORD, is my strength and my song; he has become my salvation."

Though things seem cloudy and dark at times, remember—it is a matter of *trust* and *obedience*. If it seems to be nonsensical, remember---I test in ways that man thinks is foolish---even to the confounding of simple man.

Have you been *used* and *abused* by the selfishness of others---even past disappointments from family members and others close to you?

Have your natural abilities been trampled on leaving you with the feeling of hopelessness? O My child---take your eyes off man and focus them on Me!

Come to the 'water of life' (Jesus) and learn from My Word that I AM your father and care deeply for you. I AM closer than a brother—even residing within you. But your disobedience at times keeps Me at arm's length. Trust---My child, is a matter of the *will*: impossible in your own strength to accomplish. You can---by your own ascent---do so without feelings. Put all your cares, your past and present failures, into My hands---and by your *naked will*---leave them all to Me.`

Now, minute by minute if need be, say, *"O Father sooth my brow with the touch of Your hand. Teach me to trust Your ways. For I long to be free from the chains that binds me, each link forged by my unbelief and disobedience!"*

"I in sincere honesty stand before Your throne. I have no one to blame for these chains but me! For I sought relationships---fame and yes, even riches, with the wrong attitude."

"But now I come to You in humility, realizing, that even these words that I speak now---from deep within me--- acknowledge that I, speaking by the Holy Spirit within me, am paving the way for a realized trust in Your ways."

I praise You. I thank You. I bless and glorify Your name. Worthy is the Lamb that was slain. (Rev.3:12) Thank You

241

that you place my feet upon the path of righteousness, peace, and joy in the Holy Spirit. (Rom. 14:17)

I look for Your continued teaching to grow me into maturity through Your Word and constant presence within me. Even so, come quickly Lord." (Rev. 3:11)

Now, dear child, I speak to you: I test in ways that man thinks are foolish---even to the confounding of simple man. When My timing for you is ready---I will remove the clouds of darkness from your heavy heart. Watch the circumstances that I will bring about to bring you *peace* and *joy*.

Continue in obedience to My *will* and I will show you exactly what to do. Remember the little song that says, in part---"Trust and obey, there is no other way...."

ABBA

TRUST MY LEADING

Ps. 37:3
Trust in the LORD and do good; dwell in the land and enjoy safe pasture.

Why do you whistle in the wind? Listen and see the wind blowing through the trees. See how the young leaves hang on.

Vital sap speeds through the veins and fibers of each young leaf. They look and act as if they will cling forever with their own vitality; so busy, primping—beautifully contoured, but—dusk comes, sunlight dims, the leaves lose their color—strength and drive!

So it is with Man; you seek to obey—you seek to believe, you seek to trust My voice, direction, and eternal message; your sensitivity is both a blessing and a curse!

I drew the pattern for your perfect sojourn on earth. The world, tainted by sin, twisted the pattern in your nature; and experience coupled with your natural affinity to sin---and your life drew a blank!

You hurt and grow weary because you try to interpret man's reaction to your work in Me. They do not realize why they dare to attack—to diminish your placement. Keep on—remain in earshot of My voice—"Vengeance is Mine, I will repay!"

Don't fret; don't be dismayed. Continue on---walk along My guarded path. We are getting close to the fork in the road which promises *strong ministry* for you and yours, a freeing-up of your time to do much 'team-work.'

Speak with all boldness—to the slaying of sinner and (straying) saint alike. See My glory, feel My joy—what riches await you: souls ushered into the kingdom, and lives strengthened, renewed and rededicated to Me!

Receive joy and victory—like a *'Dancing Wind'* blown in the direction of My choosing, landing on the oppressed and depressed, bringing a fresh hope and vitality to their own area of life—guided by My hand!

ABBA   5-14-82

Ref. Studies: Ps. 37:5—115:11—118:8—Pr. 3:5.

TUNE OUT THE DESTROYER

1 Peter 3:11
    He must turn from evil and do good; he must
seek peace and pursue it.

Tune out the destroyer. Tune in the Savior. Together you balance the *ship of faith.* Do you know that within the storm-tossed waters---I create a *great calm* in you---assurance that you belong; assurance that you and I are getting along.

There is so much to learn---so much to learn: *"How do I learn?"* you say. Christ paid it all, beloved, ---indeed He did! You were bought with a price---paid dearly by Me.

Studying is time well spent with Me---in My Word, as you pay the price to listen. Mountains are moving, dear children---mountains are moving as you pray---mountains, tall and rugged they be (strongholds). You must watch out for them!

"Where are they?" you say. Why, they are in the hearts of man, My children. But as you pray and chip away---as you praise and sing---as you glory in My name, as you raise your hands and voice in song---as you do these things, My child, the *stony hearts* within man crack and crumble---crack and rumble---break and shake, then the loosening begins for him and her---and for nature all about. Now *cast them out,* speaking the Word ---*in My name!*

"We have built strong and supportive *wills* to enhance our fortress," they say---but *only to their hurt!*

But as you pray---O, dear darling ones,---as you pray, using the scriptures, cracks will appear. Even their best (self-made) armor is smeared---and the process begins.

Renovated hearts burst forth with all the pomp and ceremony befitting a prince.

Majestic lights start their dance of victory over him who continues to become *non-descript* in his nature (humbled).

Watch and pray beloved---the game is not over or totally won; but one-on-one, as you pray the words---to the tearing down strongholds within each *tormented breast*---they will come to Me *for rest.* (2 Cor. 10:4)

Yes---one-on-one until final victory in that glorious day, when the final battle for man is won. Carry on, precious petals. I preserve---guard---and protect you; protecting your earnest prayers and praises as they are swept up to My throne room---like sweet smelling perfume!

TWO HEARTS BLENDED AS ONE

Psalm 27:1
> The LORD is my light and my salvation-- whom shall I fear? The LORD is the stronghold of my life-- of whom shall I be afraid?

Two hearts blended as one in Me is an unbeatable team; you walk not through a *wilderness this day.* You two are an open road filled with light, life, and colorful fields of sweet-smelling flowers, birthed, and grown with the energy given by the power of My strong right hand of fellowship.

Using My authority, go, and win over the who-so-ever-wills that have been gifted to you daily in your walk of service in My name.

ABBA

YOUR FINANCES USE AS I DIRECT

Matthew 5:42
> Give to the one who asks you, and do not turn away from the one who wants to borrow from you.

You have seen only a very small portion of the finances that I have been sending to you and yours . . . use them as I direct.

Be very alert to the needs of others this day---and the days to follow. Bring them into remembrance of Me.

Show them, by example, how to walk in the light of obedience, repentance, patience, and persistence---the four foundational pillars upon which I build a firm *core of stability* for a balanced service to Me, cemented in place with the mortar of faith and trust!

Cast all your cares upon My strong shoulders. This world continues in its decline!

Partner with Me in holding back the forces of evil until that day when I will say, "Enough—enough return to the Father of Light in preparation for the banquet to come . . . There, once again: "I will gird Myself . . .and serve you!"

ABBA

Matthew 17:27

"But so that we may not offend them, go to the lake and throw out your line. Take the first fish you catch; open its mouth and you will find a four-drachma coin. Take it and give it to them for my tax and yours."

Matthew 19:21

Jesus answered, "If you want to be perfect, go, sell your possessions and give to the poor, and you will have treasure in heaven. Then come, follow me."

YOUR HIGH AND LOFTY WORDS

1 Cor. 2:16

For who has known the mind of the Lord, that he may instruct him? But we have the mind of Christ.

Your high and lofty words of praise, adoration, and worship have been borne along with the fire of your angels to the *Mercy Seat* of My Throne ---like wings of sweet essence to My nostrils.

Know, dear ones, that I respond directly to your acts of faith and trust. I guide you through the *mine fields* of this world's torments brought on by *hateful people,* sinners known and unknown; they are but instruments of hell's thrusts and are governed by the god of this world.

Take heed! Close *any crack* in your armor with prayer, lest the enemy find a foothold and dare to come in, and create havoc!

ABBA

YOUR WORLD OF WONDERMENT

Philip. 1:27
> Whatever happens, conduct yourselves in a
> manner worthy of the gospel of Christ. Then,
> whether I come and see you or only hear about you
> in my absence, I will know that you stand firm in
> one spirit, contending as one man for the faith of the
> gospel.

Your world of *wonderment* has only begun for the tasks that I have set before you to do in My *mighty name.*

You are in a place now, as you have confirmed your *feelings of deadness* in honest repentance; for this, I bless you beyond measure.

Even today as you *live in Me* . . .My Spirit has full flow in every part of your being: spirit, soul, and body.

The words that I speak through you will bring *peace to all* within the sound of your voice.

247

Deep seated sin will be released from those you touch with your presence today; for you, blessed one, have the mind, and power of God within you to speak truth, in love, to all the who-so-ever-wills---more so from this day forward, as never before---in your long journey of the *hope* that is within you.

So be strengthened and fortified to carry out each assignment I AM pleased to give you!

ABBA

Romans 15:6
...so that with one heart and mouth you may glorify the God and Father of our Lord Jesus Christ.

Eph. 3:16
I pray that out of his glorious riches he may strengthen you with power through his Spirit in your inner being...

Col. 1:11-12
Being strengthened with all power according to his glorious might so that you may have great endurance and patience, and joyfully giving thanks to the Father, who has qualified you to share in the inheritance of the saints in the kingdom of light.

YOUR WRATH KINDLED

Psalm 76:10
Surely your wrath against men brings you praise, and the survivors of your wrath are restrained.

Rail upon the earth! ---Rail upon the sea! Quicken man's hearts; make them see. Make them know that they are homeward bound. Make them know that in Me they become sound.

Capture the unlovely---capture them for Me. It is within your commission---it is within your scope of prayer. Come settle upon man's disposition; bring him out of despair.

Loose his heart from the snare of him who binds him tight---the snare of him who gives no light. O loose him, My brother---loose him for Me.

Draw fuel from My fire. Have done with impotent prayer. Raise your sights toward heaven, and by your inner man stand in My presence---My light bathing your body.

I commission you to deliver man from his self-made plans. Kneel, praise, and pray. Stand fast in the gap, dearest one, there are so few who are willing to spend the time in *intercession* for man.

You are duty-bound to set them free in me. Honor every prayer request---immediately! I have given you the authority and power to overcome the enemy's darts; never stop short until you sense the power of the Spirit honoring your petition!

The call is clear; the call is direct. Be their truest friend. Always be instant in prayer, now go and conquer in My name.

Know in your heart of hearts that the Holy Spirit rules and reigns in your very being, watching over you along with My warrior angels to protect you from the wiles of the devil!

ABBA   6-25-83

ZOE – THE GOOD LIFE

Jn.10:10
    ....I have come that they may have life, and
have it to the full.

This, loved one, is the blessed life that satisfies man's longing heart. I have, in every man, imbedded this Zoe life into the very core of all mankind

But it is not necessarily a life of ease! What you count as drudgery can become a blessing. Even your *interruptions,* which so often trouble you and can be perturbing, are My *opportunity* to serve and use you ---in your time of greatest need!

Come to Me in prayer and meditation; come to Me for heaven-sent rest. Come to Me and experience a life that counts toward the building of the Kingdom in Heaven.

Pause and ask yourself, *"What do I want to do with my life? Help me Lord to prioritize my drives and aspirations of my life here on earth.*

Serving You is my greatest desire---spending my life in thinking about my needs---not my wants?

Help me to be a good steward of my time and talents. I want to try the Zoe life"!

My child---follow My daily direction for your life and you will never regret it as you sense My nearness.

I will help you to stay on course and live out your life for Me. (Luke 12:32) "Do not be afraid, little flock, for your Father has been pleased to give you the kingdom. Sell your possessions and give to the poor. Provide purses for yourselves that will not wear out, a treasure in heaven that will not be exhausted, where no thief comes near and no moth destroys."

Live out your life *above* your circumstances, and in so doing---you become an example of kingdom living to all who cross your path, and when I call you home---I will say, "Well done, O good and faithful servant,--- well done!"

ABBA   9- 8-09

Christ Our Joy

PART TWO

THE GREAT COMMISSION
(FOR SUCH A TIME AS THIS)

John 17:18 Net/Eng
    As You sent Me into the world, I also have sent them into the world.

Be on the alert! Satan comes to kill, tear down, and steal you away; our mission he knows not! His only concern—make you to stray!

Stay close, My love, stay close. Read and pray, read and praise Me more. Prepare your heart—concentrate on our mission; there is much work to be done for My love.

We start with you. You have been prayed for from your very beginning---you were birthed with a prayer for servitude and great faith and trust in the Holy Spirit's leading.

Ignorant people of My ways brought you along through your early years; but their love was true! Hush now—be quiet in the still wee hours, for in these wee still hours we commune, one to another!

I tapped on your heart from the very start. O! How I tried to break through. What terrible clay idols got in your way, and Mine; but the glorious majestic *Hound from Heaven* gave all mankind a start when He sent Me from the highest heaven.

I paid it all—it is complete. I tapped---I blasted that very door that stood between us, My love. Think back now, how many times you were saved from *cashing in* and wanted to quit! It was I, it-- was Me, and your Angel standing by--longing to help; watching you cry out in despair, wanting a better life—sensing that a *special call* was placed upon your life. *"O world—O! World, stop turning, stop*

253

spinning; what purpose---despair? What purpose my body broken in poor health at times? O! Don't You care that I exist? O! Don't You really care for me?"

O! My child, My Father was good, my Father was and is loving and kind. We were there all the time, your angel and I. Finally you connected the *name* with Me.

For 'I AM' the way, the truth, and the life: the anointed Son of God.

I AM the *original branch*; for out of Me you were broken, out of Me you were healed; for out of Me you came to Me of your own free will.

Your fears became sin and throttled you so; your fears of rejection were complete. But from life's crushing defeats---out of the *ash heap* you came, bent low, and on bended knee you said, *"I love You Lord---I love You indeed---I was blind, but now I see; my life I give to thee."*

O! What joy! What swelling emotion of love! For that long awaited hour struck out across the expanse of time and was recorded in His Book: "Our child has found his way— our child is clean at last! Washed in Your blood."—O! Son O! Daughter of Mine, robed in a curtain of love made white by the Lamb, take your stand, put on your mantle of prayer- -- check all your armor--- check it twice!

You and I —we march together—yes, you and I –We soar. Let us check that land to the North—what do we find? Why their angels are *ready*, if only they knew; their angels are ready—but only a few been activated by prayer!

Check your list—who now comes to mind? Stop just now, beloved: Take your pen in hand; from where you sit or stand—bring those loved ones into view.

See them with your inner eye; now write their names and *caption it*: North. Now write down their names for Me and cover their lives by My blood; I'll wash them and make them clean.

O! Don't fret—don't stew—I'm sure you've left out a few; leave room to expand your list; now eyes to the East—need a better view?

Peak through My wings—see, we are about to land. All seems well there! Quiet yourself through Me; now once more take up your pen and write. That's right, just write them down on My wing; of course, for the moment, pressed wood (paper) is all you have?

But as you press the pen against the parchment, it is immediately transferred by My hand; for My wings are large enough to cover the entire universe—O! Writer of this story!

Give them all a taste of My Glory; for out of 'Beulah land,' the battle rages---the clapboards sound. Satan is on the run, for thunderous sounds from heaven bring forth the 'former and latter rain'!

Tell them how it *pitter patters*—tell them it is more than rain; for teeming tingling raindrops, each one formed from dust, are the *pitter patter* of angels' feet rushing to complete their task, for the rain is purified as fine glass.

The rain is purified indeed! You tell them by these simple words as they pray and praise Me more that "*I make all things new.*"

Quietly, dear one, ever so quietly---*careful now*—you've brushed against an angel—you may have brushed against two!

Write down the names of those to the East. Cross over continents if you must; write them down and pray.

Now cover their lives by My blood; I'll wash them and set them free. Free to see Me as their king and Savior. Free to bow their bended knees; for remember, nothing is impossible for Me when we share our prayers together!

The burdens become light as a feather even from one of My wings. Hush now, don't fuss; again you have left out many—it's true; but what's the rush –when in your thoughts they come. Pick up your brush and add them to your Eastern list.

The night brings forth dimly lighted shadows—is it night in your soul when We turn South.

Fires from the very gates of Hell disturb this southern land; rest your eyes upon My Word---it is fitting that We say it here when pondering upon this hemisphere. "He has blinded their eyes, and hardened their hearts. Lest they should see with their eyes, lest they should understand and be converted, and I should heal them."

How true—how true that is, beloved! We have much work to do. O! I love the way you are willing to *stand in the gap* and reduce that *fallen angel* (Satan) to his designated place.

For his hands are filled with the blood of victims trampled under his feet, then picked up and thrown aside; yes, some even died because of his lies!

Agree with Me just now; for you and I with your angels form a mighty army—totally aflame with righteous anger--- kindled from our Father's throne.

O! We are not alone—not alone indeed. We are anchored in space by the Trilogy of Heaven, who bring forth leaven, leaven that soothes and heals. My wings expand—My wings beat strong. Winds all about now form into a mighty whirlwind; you, dear one, to you it is given to direct its path; O! cut a swath wide and deep—O cut one across that land.

Are you now ready? Please be steady—Here I'll take you by the hand. Isn't it grand as you write their names— O! Yes, don't forget to name the land in each list you write, for the people and the land are mated together.

There now, that wasn't so hard—now cover their lives by My blood. I'll wash them and make them clean.

Go over your lists again and again lest the demons cast out enter into those vessels made clean by My Word!

You keep them out by prayer and praise as We repair the breach with *flame;* we have been to the North—We have been to the East. We saturated the South by prayer.

Pause and lift your hands in praise—pause and take a drink from the well that never runs dry. All right, ready, we now fly West, here again another test for your inner eye! You know by now, O! Lover of Mine, that this trip is not for children. Quiet yourself—take your time. Once again you must prepare a list.

Give thought and care as you prepare whom just now comes into mind. Once again I bear them up with My new covenant of Blood; washed clean they are and dear to My heart; for remember, I too prayed in that garden of old with boldness. I *claimed them* there that none would be lost— but the son of perdition.

That was a tragic loss, and last but not least—My precious Far East, a land where you once again must spend more time; precious cargo there.

Pray that they stay in the hollow of My hand; people and the land together; light as a feather they are—gracious but cunning they be. Pray them into the kingdom strong! Pray them there for Me!

Did you write it down, names and land? I'll wait until you do; they too are under the blood. Time to bring you home for a rest, wherever your home may be.

We soared around the globe together, just a little taste of things yet to come! Pause now My son, my daughter, take a well-earned rest; until—until the morrow; then We take off to yet another test.

List after list you must compile---so take their names. Their land flows before Me like the river Nile, until one day We bring all things to a halt; when all who will be saved is caught. Rest, now precious child, rest---rest---rest upon your Father's breast.

ABBA   8-7-83

Alphabetical Listing of Titles

PART ONE

Casual Acquaintance
Changed Lives Prove Ministry
Cleanse Your Temple
Come Sit with Me
Come Walk with Me Today
Coming Into the Light
Continue to Meet the Challenges
Crooked Paths Made Straight
Danger of Shrinking Back
Deep Seated Anger
Despitefully Used
Directions for Running the Race
Disobedient Child
Divine Grace
Do Not Fear What Man Can Do
Do You Have a Zeal for God
Do You Hear the Call
Do You Want to be Made Well.
Earthbound No More
Empowered By The Spirit
Endure God's Chastening
Extended Time
Fast and Pray Before Any Mission
For a Very Special Lady
Fortified Strongholds
Fortify Yourselves
God Holds Your Breath in His Hands
God's Aim for the Church
God's Reason for Our Suffering
Greater Works Shall you Do
Guardian Angels
Hallowed Hands--Hallowed Heart
Hands That Oppose You
Harvest Time

Have You Caught The Vision
He Brought Us Out
Healed By God Alone
Healing the Mind and the Body
Health on the Morrow
His Hand Extended
Holy Words of Instruction
How Dare I say I Surrender Not
I Am An All Consuming Fire
I Bring Joy and Victory
I Long to Have You Beside Me
I Will Show Mercy on Whom I Will
If One Does Not Obey God
In Need of a Time Out
In Nothing be Anxious
In the Land of the Lord
In Times of Stress or Need
Inclination to Sin
Incline Your Hearts to Understanding
Indwelled By My Spirit
Internal Wickedness and Dishonesty
Jesus Reveals His Death and our Reward
Keep Claiming Your Healing
Keep to the Path
Keep Your Eyes on the Prize
Kept By the Power of God
Kept in the Hollow of His Hand
Let Everything be Done Decently
Let God Work in Your Life
Let the Captives Go Free
Life Provides No Short Cuts
Look After Each Other
Lord Purify My Heart
Makers of Peace

Man in Trouble
Man's Inhumanity To Man
Marvels of the Universe
Ministry of Compassion
Mirror My Father
Missionary Preparedness
My Invitation To the World
My Plans For You Never Fail
My Salvation Is Increased In You
Name Above All Names
Natural Man and Spiritual Man
Nature's Best
Nature's Way Without Help
Neglectful Children
New Beginnings - New Challenges
Nightly Tears - Joy Filled Mornings
No Real Understanding
No Small Step
Note the Upright Man
Nothing Too Hard For God
Occupy Till I Come
Offenders Will Be Punished
On The Basis of Faith in His Name
Open Prayers Sent My Way
Our God Is a Consuming Fire
Our God Works For Us
Out of the Depths of Our Poverty
Out With the Old
Overcoming Chinks
Partnered With Me
Partners on Your Way
Passing Through the Veil
Paths of Service the Same
Perfect Peace and Trust

Practice Your Hospitality
Preparedness
Raised to Higher Ground
Reach Beyond the Temporal
Rebellious Resistance
Renewed To a Place of Sonship
Repairers of the Breach
Resist His Destructive Ways
Rest in the Land of the Lord
Return Under My Protection
Rowing Without A Paddle
Salvation by Grace Alone
Say a Word To The Indifferent One
Seek Everlasting Relationship
Seek My Face O Drooping Branch
Sense the Mission Waiting Ahead
Sensing His Presence
Shepherd to the Sheep
Show Me Your Way
Sign Posts
Sin is Settled
Sing a Song of Worship
Skin Deep
Soak in the Word
Sons and Daughters of the Light
Sound Judgment - Assures Victory
Sown A Perishable Body
Speak to the Darkness
Stand and Be My Witness
Stand Fast in the Lord
Stand in the Center of My Will
Stand Midst the Storm and Strife
Stay Away From Loving Money
Stay Focused

Stay on the Course
Stretch Forth Your Hand
Strive to Enter His Rest
Submission Through Forgiveness
Take Heart
Take Your Healing Without Cost
Taste the Water Just Now
Temporary Pain
That Pearl of Great Price
The Battle Rages On
The Bondage of Sin Broken
The Chair of Agreement
The Danger of Unforgiveness
The Day of Wine and Roses
The Former and the Latter Rain
The Grapes are Ripe for Picking
The Hearing Ear and the Seeing Eye
The Lord of the Moments
The Lord's Supper
The Ministry of Compassion
The Never Failing God
The New Dispersion
The Plane of Your Imaginations
The Pot is Boiling
The Power and Authority of his Name
The Raging Storm Within
The Refining Still Goes On
The Relationship of Believers
The Saints and the Seedlings
The Secret of God Given Wealth
The World Is In Need of Cleansing
There is a Day Coming Soon
There is No Higher Calling
Thirsty Come to the Water and Drink

This is the Way Walk in It
This New Place of Rest
Those Who Would Follow Me
Three Anchors To Your Faith.
Times of Testing
To the Victor Belong the Spoils
To Whom Can You Compare
Transferring Elijah's Mantle
Trials and Tribulations
Trials and Tribulations Build Character
Trials Will Plague You in Ministry
Troubled and Disturbed Shepherds
Troubled Storm Tossed Waters
Troubled Waters
True Love
Trust His Ways
Trust My Leading
Tune Out the Destroyer
Two Hearts Blended as One
Until That Day of Disaster Comes
Walk As Children of Light
Walk in Newness of Life
We Walk By Faith
Weep Not Be Comforted
When Adversity Comes
When Disturbing News Comes Your Way
When In Doubt Or Confused
Why O Why Do My Children Cry
Will You Walk An Extra Mile
Winning Souls for the Father
Witness-Witness-Witness
Wounded Though You Be
You Are Always Thinking of Us Lord
You Have Come Into the Light

You May Feel Diminished
You Must Be Born Again
You Say You Have Faith
You Walk Not Alone
You Walk Not In the Wilderness
You Who Are Part of My Remnant
You Who Refuse the Spirit's Call
Your Beckoning Call
Your Finances Use As I Direct
Your High and Lofty Words
Your World of Wonderment
Your Wrath Kindled
Zoe The Good Life